ID0316329

Greenlaw

~~~

An

Ancient

County Town

~~~

Greenlaw – An Ancient County Town

First Edition

*no part of this book may be reproduced in any form
without the prior consent of the author.*

ISBN : 978-1-326-28503-6

©2015 James Denham

*published by Glenmore Books
www.glenmorebooks.yolasite.com*

This book is dedicated to the people of Greenlaw

*with the proceeds dedicated to the Greenlaw Festival Trust
Registered Charity No. SCO41426*

Format by Elizabeth W. Paterson

- Introduction -

*T*he story behind this booklet is, would you believe? an idea which came to me during my research in Greenlaw as part of a Duns and district book. The more I researched and the more I conversed with a very helpful lady, Carol Trotter, the more I realised, Greenlaw deserved somewhat more than being just a 'bit part' in the other book.

*T*hough I knew some of Greenlaw's distinguished past, I did not realise the depth of history which engulfed the wee place. My interest grew and grew, until I realised I had truly arrived in one of the most historic communities in Berwickshire.

I have, of course, been to Greenlaw before as part of my 'Village Kirks of the Scottish Borders' effort, when I met the good minister, Rev. Tom Nicholson, a friendly, courteous and very helpful man. The parishioners of the burgh are very fortunate to have such a man in their midst and, while this effort shows a little more definition than the Kirks' book, it is by no means an ultra definitive book.

*L*ater, during my research, I had the pleasure of meeting Doug Smith having been directed to him by the parents of Megan Muir, the Greenlaw Maid. Their words were "What Doug does not know about Greenlaw, is not worth knowing" and so right they were, I offer a big thank you to them, and, of course Doug and his wife.

I must add, Greenlaw will still be part of the Duns book, after all, a book on Duns would hardly be complete without Greenlaw considering their interchanging histories over the centuries as the County Town of Berwickshire. You will notice too, how often I refer to Greenlaw as a town, that is simply because, any community which has been granted the title *Burgh of B*arony, in my eyes, is a town, regardless of size or population.

*L*et me say, there is a little unavoidable duplication, jumping to and forth, in the book and, almost certainly, the inevitable typing errors for which I take full responsibility. Finally, If I have caused offence to any person, whether alive or dead, then I am truly sorry but really, no maliciousness is meant to anyone in any shape or form...........................

Yours Truly,

James Denham

- Acknowledgements -

I really must thank

Carol Trotter for all her help, encouragement and old photographs not to mention her enormous input in to this publication
Doug Smith for exactly the same reasons
Mamie Ede for her kind help
Rev. Thomas Nicholson for his gracious help in the past
Walter Baxter for his photographs and his words of wisdom now, and in the past. James TM Towill who also donated a photograph as did Becky Williamson. (Becky, like Walter Baxter, James T M Towill and myself, are all members of the Geograph Project, the most educational photography project in the country}

More appreciation must be given to Lee Davies and Leanne Johnston for the use of their photographs and, finally to everyone else I spoke to during my research in the town, on the streets and in Poppy's Coffee Shop

I must not forget the girls in Earlston and Galashiels libraries and the members who look after visitors at the Borders Family History Society's Research Centre in Galashiels

**Photographs from the Wikipedia Project are reproduced under the Creative Commons
Attribution ShareAlike 3.0 unreported 2.5 Generic 2.0 Generic 1.0 Generic license
(Wikimedia Commons)**

**Every photograph reproduced from the Geograph
project is under the Creative Commons Attribution ShareAlike 2.0 Generic license
furthermore, all photographs shown with credit are copyright of the author.**

- Contents -

The Historic Sign

holds out the hand

of welcome to all

from near and far

- Greenlaw -

- Early Struggles -

*T*his opening section is necessarily short since so little is known from the pre history of the region but it would appear that Greenlaw followed a similar path to Duns almost to the letter. Early inhabitation by hill dwellers, who would build the first settlement on the Law, a 'visit' from the Romans and further attacks and domination from the Angles, Saxons, Danes, Northumbrians and later, the more friendly faces of the early Apostles of Lindisfarne offering some solace to the hard pressed people on the Green Law, around a mile south of the present town. So many finds over the years, both north at Blackcastle Rings, Kaimes, Heriots Dyke, and Rumbleton, and to the south where more ancient earthworks have been found along with the site of an ancient fort at Chesters, quite clearly showing there was much early habitation and visitation while even more digs produced more evidence of Roman activity and of the English presence. In later times, Edward I 'visited' the area as did Edward III during his *Burnt Candlemas* sorties and there is absolutely no doubt, what remained of the old church was destroyed. Hertford was another who ravaged the town, church and castle during Henry VIII's *Rough Wooing* of the Scottish Court and, in time, the town, like Duns, moved from the eminence of the law to the

Blackcastle
Rings
courtesy of
Walter
Baxter
©2009

flatter lands above the Merse. It became the county seat for Berwickshire in the 15th century when Berwick was finally annexed by the English. While the county dignities swayed between the two towns over the centuries, Greenlaw held the honour for much longer than Duns, but, in 1904, it finally rested with Duns until the end of the county system in the 1990s.

There is legend, with foundation, of an old burial place to the east of Old Greenlaw which has led historians of yesteryear to believe a church existed from as early as the 7th century and if proof was needed, St. Bede, the Venerable, made mention of that ancient church in 700AD. Christianity was spreading forever northwards in to south-eastern Scotland from Lindisfarne, and Greenlaw would be one of the earliest 'recipients' of a place of worship in Berwickshire.

- Medieval Times to the the 19th century -

One of the first written notes of the existence of the area came in the 11th century when Gospatric of Dunbar was granted so much lands in the region by Malcolm III, yet another patch of Berwickshire and East Lothian, the powerful Northumbrian family had received since their arrival in Scotland; the grants were ratified by David, Prince of the Cumbrians (David I) in the early 12th century. It is not certain when the first church was erected on the site of the present but we know of William de Greenlaw granting the church and the tithes of the mill to the monks of Kelso Abbey in 1147. At that stage, Greenlaw Church had dependent chapels, at Lambden and Halyburton which were also confirmed to Kelso by William de Lamerton (perhaps Lambden) while another chapel, Rowiestone, is thought to have been granted to Melrose. We are fortunate indeed to know of so many people and charters of gifts from those early times but that simply adds to the town's importance since the beginning.

There is mention of a man known as Nigel, a parson, who appeared to 'double' as a lieutenant under Earl Patrick in the mid 12th century while another note was of William de Greenlaw, Master of the town, in a charter of lands in 1180. While that William in question, it has to be emphasised, was not a member of the Cospatric family, it is believed, some of Cospatric's immediate descendants also adopted the name of the settlement. William Grahame, the town's master and parish chaplain, who owned much lands around the town and even larger tracts near Hassington, was a very busy man who ended his days as a canon at Glasgow Cathedral. Many more names are known from those early days of expansion - there is Robert of Greenlaw who was a clerk of Master William and Roland of Greenlaw who was William's father, a burgess of the town, a laird in his own right and a very interesting character as we shall see in the churches section. Matthew de Greenlaw was the Mayor of Berwick who swore fealty to Edward I in 1296 as did Nicholas de Camb or Camp, the Vicar of Greenlaw. Others included another Matthew who was a leading Burgess in Kelso and yet another William who was said to be in attendance at Roxburgh during an English attack around the time of the fealty performances at Berwick in 1296. Another man of Greenlaw, Ralph, was Abbot of Dunfermline towards the end of the 13th century. Other notables of the parish and who also performed the act of fealty at the Hammer's feet were, Henry de Haliburton, described as a tenant of the king and his sister-in-law, Alice, wife of Phillipe de Haliburton de la counte du Berewyke. Another with association was David de Bernham, Bishop of St. Andrews and Chancellor of Scotland, who consecrated the church at Greenlaw on 2nd April, 1242 and, though it is not recorded, he would almost certainly have dedicated the building to St. Helen as at Auld Cambus to the north. Sceptics may say St. Helen has no connection with the church and burgh but there is indeed, as we are soon to find out. One more notable of those early days was Henry de Lambden who was Abbot of Kelso for 15 years in the 12th century and from a later era, Sir John Halyburton who was vicar of Greenlaw Kirk in 1478.

*T*he Cospatric family held much lands in the area and were thought to have built a tower-house at Whiteside though probably only using it for visits preferring to live at Hume Castle following their assumption of that name. Other proprietors in the parish were the Broomfield (or

Broumfield) family, the de Cranstons of Old Greenlaw, the Redpath family, the Hatelys and the Heryns. The Redpaths were the principal lairds at Old Greenlaw but were succeeded by the Cranstons, while in the early days of the 'new' Greenlaw, the Broomfields appeared to hold sway.

Greenlaw Castle is thought to have been built in the 13th century by William de Greenlaw (of the Dunbar family) who assumed the name of the settlement. William, and his wife Ada, (his cousin) also owned Hume Castle **(left)** which had been a gift to Ada from her father, and from that couple, William and Ada, the noble family of Home were descended though others believe it was from Patrick, second son of Cospatrick, a century earlier.

The Castle later passed in to the hands of the de Cranston family who received the original honour of Greenlaw, as a Burgh of Barony by James II in the early 15th century but it would appear, there is some confusion regarding that grant, was it Burgh of Barony or simply Barony? Whatever the case, it is of no consequence since the Cranstons resigned the barony in 1598 in favour of Sir George Home of Dunbar, High Treasurer of Scotland who almost certainly extended Greenlaw Castle on the right bank of the Blackadder Water near Castle Mill. In his address, while erecting George Home to the Baronetcy, King James VI made mention of his church of St. Helen of Greenlaw. While now the owner of Greenlaw Castle, George Home, Earl of Dunbar rarely stayed there, most of his time was spent, at Whitehall in London in his principal role as Chancellor of the Exchequer; George died in 1611 and his body interred in Dunbar Church where a large monument stands in his honour. Other members of the Hume or Home dynasty who were beginning to make their mark, were the Humes of Polwarth later Lords of Polwarth and Earls of Marchmont who lived at Redbraes before building the elegant Marchmont House (**see, Where the Lairds lived**) Another great house in the parish, was Tenendrie or Tenandry of which very little is known apart from the fact, George, Earl of March granted it to his armour bearer, George Inglis in 1422 but was later in the own of the Broomfield family.

*A*nne Home, daughter of Sir George, the new baron, and her husband, Sir James Home of Cowdenknowes, were the next keepers of the Barony and castle before it passed to their great nephew, Sir Alexander Home of Manderston. Greenlaw Castle stayed in that family, until at least 1730, when it was deserted, later to become part of a farm complex and was finally demolished in the mid 19th century. All that remains of the great fort is a mound in the middle of a field.

*F*rom the latter part of the 15th century, the Kirktoun of Greenlaw had become the main centre of population, the parish town and county town of Berwickshire. It must be said however, both communities at Greenlaw, old and new, existed side by side for some centuries while others believe, the move from old to new happened, more or less,

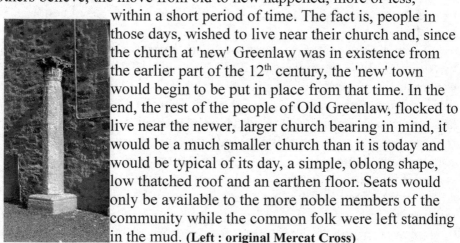

within a short period of time. The fact is, people in those days, wished to live near their church and, since the church at 'new' Greenlaw was in existence from the earlier part of the 12th century, the 'new' town would begin to be put in place from that time. In the end, the rest of the people of Old Greenlaw, flocked to live near the newer, larger church bearing in mind, it would be a much smaller church than it is today and would be typical of its day, a simple, oblong shape, low thatched roof and an earthen floor. Seats would only be available to the more noble members of the community while the common folk were left standing in the mud. (**Left : original Mercat Cross**)

- Medieval times to the 19th century -

A market cross was erected signifying the right to hold markets and fairs and the Baron, who was granted those rights, ordered the fairs to be held twice yearly, one of which, to be held on the feast day of the town's patron, St. Helen; the fairs and markets were held round the new market cross on the village green until 1870. A common hall (town hall) too, was built for meetings regarding the burgh and county business long before the days of the new county hall. In much later times, when that new hall we now see, was being built, the cross was removed to the kirk, and lost, but happily it was later re-found and placed, at the west gable of the church tower though without the Lion Rampant pinnacle, while a new cross was erected in front of the new hall. Barely a century later, the county privileges passed to Duns but, when the new baron, Patrick Hume, Lord Polwarth and 1st Earl of Marchmont arrived, he 'put things right' and Greenlaw was soon restored to what was perceived as its rightful status in 1696 and over the next century and more, the population of the town increased and a school opened.

*A*s the county seat, Greenlaw was also home to county justice and a tiny jail was built for those who weren't executed. The jail was much too small for purpose but an answer was found in 1712, to build a tower like structure at the west gable of the kirk **(above)** The 'church tower jail' was soon built and still remains to the present day, complete with iron barred gate and iron grilled windows, a grim sight indeed considering it is now joined to a place of worship. Still it is unique and is one of the iconic attractions of the town; a court house was later added to the tower but that has long since been demolished. The miscreants who were found guilty at court, now had no need to walk far to receive their punishment, only a few steps to the jail, or in to the kirkyard where they would be executed by hanging. Perhaps hanging would be have been kinder to some since the jail had a gruesome reputation and soon became known as *Hell's Hole* or *Thieves' Hole* which was immortalised in rhyme :

> *"Here stands the gospel and the law*
> *wi' hell's hole atween the twa"*

County Jail of the 19th century

Courtesy of Carol Trotter

*W*hile the tower is now adjoined to the church, there is no passage from one to the other. There was a window from the tower through to the kirk allegedly to allow prisoners to view, or even take part in the service and a mark on the upper wall at the west gallery appears to confirm that. As mentioned, the court house adjoining that tower was demolished making way for a new court in the county hall while another jail, for the whole county, was later built nearby, in roughly where Bank Street is today. The jail was described in 1824, only weeks after it was built, as a 'more than adequate building' containing 18 cells for those who would be spending some time behind bars, two day rooms where books were made available to those who could read and where they were served their meals; petty criminals had their own day room but they all shared the exercise yards. The whole compound was surrounded by tall, strong walls with the jailer's house just outside the perimeter of the building. Interestingly the old jail keepers' house still stands as a private home though for many years was used as the police station.

To get some idea of how important and busy Greenlaw was, and its ability to attract more people, we just have to take a look at a directory of 1826 giving us some indication of the hustle and bustle of a busy wee town. Have a look at this impressive list of businesses etc. : A Post Office, subscription library, two baker's shops, ten grocers (five of them selling wines and spirits) four inns, eight shoemakers, four blacksmiths, five carpenters, two coopers, several smiths, twelve drapers and dress makers, hand and loom weavers, tailors and milliners, all making the end products of the farms and the linen and lint mills. The Waulk, corn and barley mills lined the River Blackadder providing more employment while other trades included bleach fields and dye houses, the list goes on and on. Another impressive directory of the town of 1881 can be viewed in Carol Trotter's fine article on the Town Hall website.

It was, at that time and beyond, an extremely busy and populous locale and was able to sustain three churches, up to four schools and two doctors. Further adding to the above were, jailers, surveyors, lawyers, watch makers, cabinet makers and the Sheriff's Officers. All the trades of the day were busy as was the daily coach between Duns and Edinburgh. Other carriers carried goods to Duns, Coldstream and Edinburgh every day while the railways came to the town in the second half of the 19th century. All forms of mills and quarries were situated all around the immediate area and were kept busy competing with others and satisfying the needs of the burghers and the wider region.

The 19th century though, was not all about development and improvement, it had its downsides too, and severe ones at that, when Great Britain became embroiled in no less than four wars, the Napoleonic Wars from 1803 to 1815, the Crimean War which was enacted from 1853 until 1856 and the two Boer Wars, the first of which lasted for a few months between 1880 and 1881 then the second, more serious affair, from 1899 until 1902. Men of every parish in the country were involved and, while Britain 'triumphed' in all those encounters, it came at great cost to both life and prosperity. After every hellish event, men came home, some whole of body and mind, some badly wounded, leaving many of their comrades behind on those bloody fields of conflict. Records of the dead are, at best, sparse or, at worst, non existent. Greenlaw was affected by all those conflicts when many of the returning heroes had no jobs to return to, particularly following the wars against Napoleon Boneparte, Emperor of France.

*H*appily, Sir William Purves-Hume-Campbell, the 6th Baronet, stepped in to the cause of helping returning heroes, fresh from their efforts at the Battle of Waterloo. There was simply no work available but Sir William had other ideas. In a great show of compassion, the local lord created work as a means of helping hard pressed families. One of the main ventures he put the men to work on was to dig a huge trench across Greenlaw south common, from roughly near the site of the Easter Bridge all the way to near the site of the railway station while other, much needed works, were provided for the men to keep them busy and earn some badly needed money. Though the wages were meagre, they were better than nothing and, of course helped put some food on the family table. There was too, from the 16th century, a poor fund which was initiated by the Heritors of the Parish, where the more wealthy of the community paid in to the fund in an effort to help the poorer in times of need.

*I*n the wake of the Napoleonic Wars and the subsequent Crimean War, the price of food rocketed, partly due to extra tax being imposed by the Westminster Government, on both industry and utility. Tobacco and alcohol were taxed for the first time and, with the recently introduced personal income tax, living and raising a family was difficult. Throughout the 19th century, the cost of living rose as never before and that was the case for some 70 years. Still, the good laird, Sir William, did try to make life a little more bearable for the people in the Parish of Greenlaw. Times were indeed hard but the 19th century proved to be the busiest century in the town thus far with much of what we now see, built during that period. Not only was there a new jail and jailer's house, the bank had arrived and the Good Templars Hall was built in what became known as Bank Street. The Good Templars was a movement formed by men who chose to abstain from alcohol and formed clubs all over the country and, while they were perceived as a 'secret society' they did provide local communities with a meeting place where they could relax, play music, dance the night away and generally enjoy themselves, without alcohol. The streets were being renewed, much new housing was built on the main thoroughfare, on the wynds leading towards the river and on the Duns and Marchmont roads.

The most iconic building in the town was built from 1828 and took three years to complete but it was three years worth waiting for; that building was the County or Town Hall. The hall, financed at a cost of £6,500 (several million pounds at today's values) by, Sir William Purves-Hume-Campbell, was built in the Greek Revival style to a design of architect, John Cunningham, and served its purpose as county headquarters and court until 1904. In that year, its days as county headquarters had come and gone, afterwards used as a community or town hall where much of the local socialising took place and, if I may fast forward, it was later used to billet Polish soldiers during World War II when it had a near miss on April 7ᵗʰ 1941 when German planes dropped bombs only yards away on the Duns Road. Another bomb was found in recent years when local people were creating a tennis court (Greenlaw lay on the route taken by German bombers heading to and from Clydebank and its shipyards) The hall was then used as a swimming pool but for many years it lay unused. In 2006, the old masterpiece was shortlisted on the BBC programme, *Restoration Village* but, while the building did not win the competition to be fully restored, it did highlight the dreadful plight of such an iconic structure. Its appearance on the show did ignite a fire of interest and soon gifts of money came flowing resulting in the old lady being restored and now, having been wholly refurbished, perhaps there are chinks of light for a brighter future, The renovations complete, the building was reopened by HRH Prince Charles, Duke of Rothesay in June 2011, to rousing approval from a large assembly, and now it is a case of finding suitable uses to maintain the building as a viable project, like letting space for offices. The regeneration of the beautiful old building, one of the most magnificent in the entire country, could mean a new beginning for the ancient village. Another Cunningham creation, Castletoun House formerly Castle Hotel which was built around the same time as the town hall, is now a private residence though side buildings are being let for offices or any other suitable business ventures. As a side note, the former Castle Hotel we knew and loved, was the second Castle Inn on the site.

Castle Hotel now a private residence

Courtesy of Lee Davies

During the 19th century, the County Hall and courthouse were the scene of countless court cases and, being the principal court of the region's justiciary, was witness to all forms of crime, from the petty to the especially serious including murder, with the powers to condemn the guilty to the ultimate sentence, death. In actual fact, the very last public hanging in Scotland took place at Greenlaw Kirk on the 2nd April, 1834 when Mannus Swinney, an Irishman, was executed for assault and robbery.

Of course, it was not all about crime or executions and happy days were had particularly at fairs and markets. More shops opened but still the travelling salesmen came to sell their wares providing competition for the local shopkeepers and offering a wider choice for the local people but not greeted with glee by the local traders.

A new school was built off the Duns Road and was joined by another school situated just off West High Street, a couple of one teacher, private schools and a Dame School. Another two churches arrived and, it is thought, two meeting houses, all joining the parish church. Last, but by no means least, the railway arrived on the Reston to St. Boswells line. That opened up a new, faster means of travel for the local people, visitors and, of course, the new, travelling traders. Greenlaw was growing and it would appear, at that point, to be on its way to a much larger town than it now is. All the facilities were in place in a community which stood on a direct route from north to the south and for a very long time, travellers did use the route as their principal means of heading in those directions with the Castle Inn, the biggest 'winner' with many stopping there for food, refreshment and perhaps, boarding for the night. Alas, at the close of the 19th century, Britain was again at war, this time in South Africa for the second time in a few years.

*T*wo of the most important statistics of the 19th century arrived in 1832 with the Reform Bill, Scotland Act and later in the century, a national survey of the cost of living. The 1832 act meant that any men in Scotland who owned a house with a rateable value of more than £10 per annum would now be able to vote at General Elections. That act meant that 65,000 Scots were now eligible for the vote compared with a miserly 5,000 before the reform. The other statistic which referred to the latter part of the century, and had more meaning to the common folk was, the huge reduction in the cost of living. Meat, wheat, barley and corn were now at lower prices than they were at the beginning of that century while wages were at an all time high. More and more workers were also now being paid in money rather than 'in kind' which felt like another pay rise. So, in a sense, at that point in the village's history, the people never 'had it so good'. That too had its benefits with more businesses opening meaning more jobs and a new found confidence. At that stage, at the turn of the 19th and 20th centuries, the county town of Berwickshire, Greenlaw, was at its peak.

- Greenlaw -

Greenlaw Railway Station

Stoddarts Store on the corner of Duns Road and the High Street

....Courtesy of Carol Trotter

**Left : David Veitch
Grocers and Wine Merchants
(now an antique shop)**

Below:

**Stepping Stones
on the Blackadder
at Wester Row**

- Greenlaw -

- Greenlaw - 20th century to present day -

*T*he 20th century began with mixed feelings for the people of Greenlaw. In 1902, the Second Boer War reached its conclusion then, two years later, in 1904, the town finally lost its county honours when they were removed to Duns for the last time. It left Greenlaw a less busy community, gone was much of the the hustle and bustle of lawyers, judges including the County Sheriff and council operatives, though still busy with travellers on one of the principal routes. Indeed, the Castle Inn was still kept busy with travellers and of course provided for the garaging of the coaches and stabling of horses. Perhaps not so grand as housing the many lawyers who attended the local courthouse, but nonetheless, busy. Even during the days of omnibus travel between Edinburgh and London, the Castle Inn was a very popular stopping point. Business too carried on as is if nothing was amiss and the employment index we witnessed earlier, was much the same in the early 20th century. Life went on for the villagers, they and their forebears had suffered four wars in less than a century but nothing could ever have prepared them for what was to come.

*O*n August 4th 1914, the British Prime Minister, Herbert Asquith, declared war on Germany after an ultimatum to the Germans to leave Belgium was ignored. Everyone in Britain waited patiently but with baited breath for that announcement which would change the world forever. Every community in Britain was to be affected and Greenlaw was no exception. During the chaos of that war, which lasted from 1914 until 1918, the small community of Greenlaw had given up no less than 32 of its young men, with more who died as a direct result of their injuries after the war. Those young laddies died for everyone, for their families, their community, county and country, they died in an effort to drive out evil and make our world a better and safer place in which to live. This was the war, the so called Great War, which would end all wars forever, but did it?

*M*ore changes to the voting laws arrived in 1918 when all men over 21 were given the right to vote with women aged over 30 also getting that right but only after taking in to account her property status. In 1929 voting was permitted to all over the age of 21 regardless of status. This all overturned the Reform Act of 1832 when only men who owned property were allowed the vote.

Greenlaw created its very own piece of Scottish Social History when, in 1922, a power station was built and opened, meaning the people of the Burgh were the first in southern Scotland to experience this important development in electricity. This all came about when a group of local businessmen led by Robert Young, came together to discuss the possibility of opening an electric power station using the power of the Blackadder at the spot where it serviced the wheels of the Waulk Mill for centuries.

In 1939, the world erupted again and Greenlaw suffered once more. As we have already seen, that war actually touched the villagers when German planes, heading home from blitzing Clydebank, offloaded bombs on Greenlaw causing damage to road and property on the Duns Road. Several planes crashed nearby during the war years in their comings and goings at Charterhall, the aerodrome just 'down the road'

Over the three centuries since the Treaty of Union in 1707, the numbers of boys who have died in the name of Great Britain and liberty is incalculable. Every town and village in Britain lost so many of their young men and a place the size of Greenlaw, particularly in the Great War, suffered disproportionately. Only 21 years after the end of that war, the war which would end all wars, the world was again, as we have seen, about to erupt and, in 1939, it did! Britain was once again at war with Germany, a war which would last for six long years. So many people across Europe were left homeless and in some cases, without a country. Poland felt the effect worse than most and countless thousands of their youth left to form the Polish Brigade in Britain, many of whom were billeted in Berwickshire, including Greenlaw and 'took over' nearly every available building including the Town Hall and many of the large houses. After the war, the Polish troops were not allowed home for fear of arrest meaning so many of them remained and lived out the rest of their lives in Berwickshire. Men of the Italian and German military were detained in prisoner of war camps on lands around Greenlaw.

- Greenlaw -

*F*our Greenlaw lads died in the Second World War, yet another four young men who died for us to help make our world a safer place but yet conflict goes on and on. There never appears to be a single decade passes without Britain being at war somewhere around the world, all in an effort to make the world 'safer' and yet, year on year, the situation seems to get worse. That now beggars the question, why did the men of Greenlaw and indeed the rest of the country, die?

*O*nly two years after the end of WWII, Greenlaw felt the full 'wrath of nature' when great waves of extremely severe weather hit the entire area. In the Winter of late 1947, Greenlaw suffered its worst snowfalls in living memory and the good folk were stranded behind drifts of up to 20 feet deep, for over a week. Thankfully, the village was self sufficient in food supplies and the butchers and bakers kept everyone well fed, hale and hearty despite the deluge. In August the following year, another great storm erupted, this time rain. The heavens opened up battering the town for nearly 48 hours causing unheard of damage sweeping away the rail bridge near the station just a minute or so after a train, full of passengers, had crossed. Many houses in the village were engulfed with well over a metre of water causing the elderly and young to be evacuated. Properties and businesses were severely damaged by flotsam crashing along the High Street and through the shops from front to back before the flooding waters finally left Greenlaw but not before taking Easter Bridge with them. In fact, the present is the fourth bridge to stand on that site. The fall of the railway bridge also meant sadly, the end of the railways. More damage was caused throughout Berwickshire in perhaps, the worst rain storm ever recorded in the county. The weather of course is not always so bad in Greenlaw and set as it is, tucked below the hills, enjoys relatively benevolent conditions most of the time.

*G*ood weather or bad, life goes unabated in the old burgh and there is so much going on; like a well established amateur football team which currently plays in the Border League, Div. B, and, as I write, the club is organising a great Party in the Park event to raise some extra funds and of course provide for an enjoyable evening.

More old photographs...

Army personnel and Post Office staff outside Greenlaw Post Office

Happer – Tailor and Clothier
Mr. George Happer at front door

....Courtesy of Carol Trotter

**County Hall and, behind left,
The bomb damage of 1941**

**Looking west
on
East High Street**

- Greenlaw -

- Greenlaw -

Then there is the welcoming bowling club, golf club, tennis club, yoga classes, a zumba group, fishing club, a branch of the Scottish Women's Rural Institute, Church Guild, Equibuddy (riding for the disabled) GR8 club for younger children, an art group, first responders, horticultural society, flower show, a 'walk it' group, the Masonic Lodge Blackadder No. 1350, and the Greenlaw Festival Trust joining so many other groups.

Quite apart from the grand old County Hall, there are other halls in the town, like the Fairbairn Hall of 1846, formerly the Free Church School and the Good Templars Hall of 1892 which changed to the War Memorial Club in 1919 but is now known simply as the War Memorial Hall and is situated in Bank Street. The hall was originally opened for the benefit of the community and following recent refurbishment after some years of decay, has been returned to its original principal and use. That hall contains a coffee shop, Poppy's, where the staff give of their time freely, and is open Tuesday to Saturday each week. There is a used book stall, a small, town museum and, of course the hall which is available for all occasions, whether it be social, educational or business and is used by some of the local clubs. There is another restaurant and chip shop, Greenlaw Restaurant, on East High Street and of course the Blackadder Hotel, Blackadder Social Club and the Cross Keys Inn.

A wee walk round the town is needed to get a 'feel' for the place and get to know some of the friendly folk. Greenlaw has a good mix of housing from what may have been old mill houses, cottages, villas, a few flats and larger town houses. There is a nice blend of private houses, social housing and the senior members of the society are well looked after with state of the art housing. Apart from the main thoroughfares, other enchanting wynds lead off the High Street, like Todholes being joined by Mill Wynd while newer streets include Fairbairn Court which was opened by HM Queen Elizabeth in July, 1994, on the site of old an old garage and petrol filling station which in turn had replaced the power station. Other streets include Church Hill, Avenue, Blackadder Crescent and Queen's Row. More fine houses can be found on the Edinburgh Road while housing on Marchmont Road and Wester Row overlook the everlasting river, a lovely setting.

Petrol station where now stands Fairbairn Court

Courtesy of Doug Smith

If ever proof was needed of this being one of the principal meeting points in the Borderlands, you have it here where six roads lead in to town from every point of the compass. The roads lead from Earlston and Gordon, from Coldstream, from Edinburgh and Lauder, the moors road from Duns, the minor road from Halyburton and finally, Marchmont Road from where you can reach Marchmont House passing some, perceived to be, ancient earthworks and the site of a Roman fort at Chesters. Many farms are situated along every route and all use the wee town for everyday shopping and social relaxation. Quite apart from what has already been mentioned, today's wee burgh contains two shops, one of them, the former Post Office, a butcher's shop, two garage businesses, an internet café, the New Palace Centre Theatre Organ Heritage Centre, where ancient cinema and theatre organs are kept, cared for and, of course played. The centre also stages film shows and is akin to a small theatre. Film shows of the silent firm era are also shown from time to time. There is a health centre and pharmacy, kiddies' play areas, a fine primary school, bed and breakfast establishment, builders, stone masons and joinery firms, an embroidery factory (Greenlaw's largest employer) speciality candle makers, organic vegetable growers, groundworks firm, haulage, painters, auction company, furniture restorers, antique shop, ice cream and snack sales, visiting bank and post office and the popular Blackadder Caravan Park which boosts the town's population for a goodly part of the year; and let us not forget the surrounding farms which still provide employment though not so much as yesteryear. We must not forget, the beautiful walks around the town, the woodlands and, of course, along the river and the flat track bed of the old, long gone railway, though the Station House still stands as a private home.

The people are extremely proud of the men who gave their lives in the two world wars and a fitting tribute honours those brave laddies at the War Memorial, which fronts a scene, which sums up the old town. The War Memorial sits in front of the Mercat Cross which, in turn is in front of the great County Building with its great columned portico and dome and, of course, the old church looming in the background. Finally there are the lands of Greenlaw mill and farm which were purchased by George Happer before he rented lands back to the farmers and gave up a field for use of the old Greenlaw Games: after his death, it all passed to WS Happer but we shall read more of that later in the notable people section.

Site of Greenlaw Free Church – The Fairbairn Kirk

**Left :
The Memorial Cairn
of 1978
and
Further dedication
of 1992
Unveiled by
Mrs Ann Trotter
daughter of
WS Happer**

**Below:
Greenlaw
Football Club
Pavilion**

…..On the right bank of the River Blackadder

A walk through the woodlands

Steps leading to the WS Happer Memorial Woodland

- Greenlaw -

Of course, another sight not to be missed is the River Blackadder itself, a stretch of water which gives name to so much in the town, such is its importance. From Wester Bridge to Easter Bridge it provides so much enjoyment to all, be they fishers, walkers or children out wading just as their forebears did for generations. The Blackadder Water rises above Westruther near the Twin Law Cairns and soon welcomes the waters of the Edgar, Wedderlie and Fangrist, all small burns. Lady Blackadder then meanders through the Merse before joining, arm in arm, with the prodigious Langton Burn near both Kimmergehame and Wedderburn Estates The waters then waltz, in exciting tandem, towards Allanton where they meet the Whiteadder which now becomes the prominent name. All the burns and waters from Westruther, Langton, Duns and Allanton, finally team up with the gracious River Tweed at Whiteadder Point near East Ord in Northumberland. The Tweed has, itself, flowed the full length of the Scottish Borders from its source at Tweed's Well near Tweedsmuir in the old county of Peeblesshire. Finally, the Blackadder and all the friends she has joined, arrive at their destination between Berwick and Tweedmouth, washing the golden sands of the Spittal beach before disappearing in to the North Sea.

Confluence of the Whiteadder and Blackadder, north of Allanton

- Greenlaw Festival -

*E*very June, the whole parish and folk from further afield, join together in a weekend of fun and laughter and enjoy the residue of the good work of the Greenlaw Festival Trust in making the Greenlaw Festival come alive as it has done for more than fifty years and this year will be no different. Everyone comes together to make the event as enjoyable as possible and it really is the highlight of the year but before the big party there has to be an Installation of the Maid night and that is another special occasion with a right old 'knees up' at the Blackadder Social Club.

*T*he Greenlaw Festival, as we know it, was inaugurated in 1960 and, apart from a couple of small breaks, has been enacted, with growing success, ever since. It is a time for sharing in a common cause to bring the community together and help make an already good place in which to live, even better, so let's join the celebrations. For several decades, before the present format arrived, the village held their professional games including cycling and athletics on the patch of land where now stands Happer Memorial Park. The games were always well attended and the fun fair was always ready and waiting on the villagers return from the park. Fun and laughter was the name of the game then, as it is now but sadly no longer, the fun fair.

*T*he principal of the Festival is the Greenlaw Maid who, until 1993, was crowned by a local dignitary but from that time, has been crowned by her predecessor. This year, 2015, the Greenlaw Maid is Samantha Hogg, the latest in the long line of proud lassies being chosen to be Greenlaw's annual 'principal'

- The full list of Greenlaw Maids -

1960...Sylvia Miller 1961...Josephine Young 1962...Janice Miller
1963...Fiona Happer 1964...Ruby Murdy 1965...Rebecca Birbreck
1965...no maid...   1966...Aileen Cockburn 1967...Wilma Miller
1968...Carol Murdy 1969...Rosie Gillie   1970...Margaret Todd
1971...Cathleen Davis 1972...Annie Chisholm 1973...Elizabeth
Patterson 1974...Margaret Luke 1975...no maid

- Greenlaw -

1976...Clarinda Mathew 1977...Diane Baxter 1978...Glenda Brown
1979...Susan Lothian 1980...Hazel Redpath 1981...Fiona Chisholm
1982...Hazel Archibald 1983...Jill Patterson 1984...Marie Sharp
1985...Yvonne Bolton 1986...Morag McLean 1987...Julie Anderson
1988...Jennifer Trotter 1989... Debbie Campbell 1990...Debbie Gillie
1991...Caroline Campbell 1992...Sharon Douglas 1993...Paula Foster
1994...Julie Foster 1995...Rebecca Kukk 1996...Cassie Murphy
1997...Michelle Ramage 1998...Gillian Trotter 1999...Emma
Learnmouth 2000...Dawn Scobbie 2001...Audrey Berwick
2002...Jemma Richardson 2003...Aynsley Smilie 2004 and 2005...no
maids 2006...(Fayre Maid)..Nicky Lothian 2008...Rebecca Watson
2009...Beth Campbell-Whitton 2010...Kirsten Canning 2011...Hannah
Hay 2012...Shannon Hirst 2013...Gwyneth Hume 2014...Megan
Muir 2015...Samantha Hogg

2013 Maid – Gwyneth Hume and her court

Above :

2014 Maid

Megan Muir

Right :

2015 Maid

Samantha Hogg

now looking forward to
her Coronation

- Greenlaw -

*O*ne of the great highlights of the festival arrives early with the installation of the *Greenlaw Maid* on the last Saturday of June each year. The Maid is usually a first year pupil at Berwickshire High School with her court made up of boys and girls from Greenlaw Primary School.

*I*t really is a great time to be in Greenlaw and though the actual festival only lasts for one weekend, it takes a year of careful planning and organisation. A more recent addition to the festival is the exciting 'Doodecacathalon' which involves teams competing through the whole month of June, that is long before and during the official Festival weekend. To get some idea of what those mad hatters (oops! Teams) get up to, take a look at their list of events ranging from the unique to normal team games, then the tricky, funny, even funnier and downright hilarious. Here is the complete list of events in 2014 : Bowling competition, 3k and 5k run or walk, cake competition, drawing and painting, then there is yum or yuk...a game of guessing what plants can be eaten and what can't. Then there is dodge the ball, football, golf, 4x4 challenge, fly an angel, human skittles, village treasure hunt, I'm a celebrity...get me out of here, invent, vaulting and the Scarecrow Open. On the Saturday night? There is the fancy dress competition and finally Greenlaw's got talent. The team which scores the most points overall wins the Wilma Moscrop Memorial Trophy.

*E*xcitement is growing as the big event draws ever nearer and nearer. Before it finally gets underway on the Thursday before the BIG weekend when all the marquees are erected and volunteers are always warmly welcomed, to help with such a painstaking operation and will be duly rewarded, if they are lucky, with a bacon butty and a cup of refreshing tea. Friday at 6.30pm heralds the beginning of the celebrations when a popular family quiz show is followed by a good, old fashioned ceilidh in the company of the Royal Scottish Country Dancers. That is a late, late show before, for the fisherfolk, an early start on the Saturday morning when the fishing competition gets going on the Blackadder at 7.00am.

- The Festival -

While that is going on, the Village Green is being prepared for the day's regal proceedings. All is in place now and everyone on the Green gives out a great big cheer for the assembled visitors, a cheer which can be heard in the surrounding hills and now, with baited breath, they await the arrival of the Maid Elect. At 12.15pm, the excited Maid leaves home to begin her journey to her Throne on the Green. Her 'State Coach' is led every inch of the way by Duns Pipe Band then at 12.30, she is crowned as the Greenlaw Maid, the festival is now officially opened before the minister, Rev. Tom Nicholson blesses the event.

Following the blessing, there is a regal procession around the Town Hall, then, from 1.15pm onwards, the scramble begins with tea and cakes in the main marquee, served with a smile by members of the Scottish Women's Rural Institute. Circus tricks, fun and games on the Green while side stalls and car boot sellers are calling out their wares.

  Meanwhile, locals and visitors are busy checking out and marvelling at the scarecrows all around the village, some of which are works of genius, providing us all with a good idea of the Greenlaw sense of humour. So many of those scary creatures though, are well thought through and creative works of art. 2.30 pm sees the arrival of fancy dress entrants and some wonderful sights are there to be witnessed and much admired.

Above: Footballer and Piper Scarecrows - Courtesy of Walter Baxter

- Greenlaw -

Soon it is 5.00pm and everyone is invited to help clear up in readiness for the evening's entertainment. That evening sees the contestants entertaining all, in Greenlaw's Got Talent, and I am assured, there really is talent in the village and is truly a show to look forward to. There is a *Bucking Bronco* event happening on the Green while the talent competition is taking place in the large marquee before being followed by a fun filled disco, again a late, late show.

Sunday, the last day of the Festival, has a much more sedate start when a family service is held in the Parish Kirk from 10.00am. Following the sermon, there is the popular Teddy Bears' Picnic and a pet show, all great fun, especially for the children. That is followed, at 2pm, by the children's sports where the younger ones of the community can compete with their friends and, as is always the case, the competition is fierce. There are even some events for adults and though that competition is not so serious as the kids, it is much more hilarious. 3.30pm sees the annual awards ceremony when the Wilma Moscrop Memorial Trophy, Lanie Purves Trophies, Marin Johnston Trophy and so many other awards being given to various categories. At last it is time for one of the highlights of the Festival, the Duck Race. Don't be surprised if you see some steam powered ducks or some with sails or even super sonic ducks, as everyone, adults and children compete fiercely for the chequered flag.

The end of another fabulous weekend comes to an end and the Festival is over for another year. Before anyone can reflect on their joy, happiness and even triumphs, it is time for the big clear up and the dismantling of the marquees which again, is a real community effort. Another Festival is over and everyone trudges home quietly, sad another weekend of fun is over but there is always next year, and the year after.......

We mentioned the Royal Scottish Dancers earlier, let me give you some background taken from the Festival Programme :

The Royal Scottish Country Dance Society was founded in Glasgow in 1923. Its object is to advance the education of the public in traditional

- The Festival -

Scottish Country Dancing and its music.
The popularity of the RSCDS grew rapidly and spread far and wide
throughout the world.
Duns and District Branch of the RSCDS was founded in 1953 and
celebrated its 60th anniversary in 2013. In 1954, the first May weekend
was held and, of course, last year, celebrated its 60th anniversary too.

The Monday after the celebration has arrived and life slowly gets back to normal but the Festival will still be on everyone's lips for weeks to come. At least the children who took part in the fun of the weekend, are on holiday from school, so no need to rise early when all they have to do for the rest of that day, and each day of the coming weeks, is to go out with their friends and have even more fun.

More Scarecrows – more fun

left:
Wish I had gone to Specsavers
Courtesy and copyright
©2014 James T M Towill

right:

Doctor Who
Courtesy and copyright
©2013 Walter Baxter

- Greenlaw -

Photographs of Today...

Footbridge
over
the
Blackadder
Water
at Wester
Row

The
river's
entry
in to
Greenlaw
under the
Wester Bridge

Fairbairn Hall
Formerly
the Free Church
School

Mill Wynd
Looking toward
the
High Street

The
War
Memorial
Hall
formerly the
Good Templars
Hall
in
Bank Street

The
Bowling
Club
and green with the
Blackadder
Caravan Park
in the background

47

- Greenlaw -

- Greenlaw – Education -

*F*rom the Reformation in 1560, it was deemed necessary to ensure every child in Scotland had access to totally free education and plans were made to found schools in every parish in the country and, though it took more than two centuries to complete, that pledge was finally achieved. In the case of Greenlaw the first dedicated school arrived in, or before, 1660, exactly 100 years after the Reformation. There seems little doubt however, the children were being educated before that time, probably in the Parish Kirk with lessons being given by the minister and his clerk. The year 1667 was the first time an official school is mentioned when Thomas Broomfield of Greenlawdean bequeathed a large sum of money to the school on his death in that year but, it is believed, the school had been open for some years before that time.

*T*he schools at Greenlaw appear to have always been situated on or near the present school. The first school was replaced in the early 19th century behind what is now the health centre situated in the old schoolhouse, and the present school in Queen's Row again, is built in much the same spot just north of the old church.

*W*e are indeed fortunate to know the names of some of the early teachers thanks to Gibson's book, *An Old Berwickshire Town, The History of the Town and Parish of Greenlaw from the earliest times,* the most in-depth catalogue of the life and times of the old Burgh.

*T*he first known schoolmaster was Patrick Christie in 1696 and he was succeeded by David Borthwick who doubled his role as school master with his other occupation, a Writer of the Bond. Mr Borthwick arrived in 1703 but died in 1717. The next known teacher was Alexander Redpath, the husband of Ann Gilliland, sister of the Minister Rev. James Gilliland. It is not known when he started in the post but we do know the year of his death, 1783. Next in line was Thomas Henderson of Gordon, a busy and popular man in village and kirk, serving, as he did as the Kirk Session Clerk and Precentor in the church as well as teaching the children. He died relatively young, in 1773 and was buried in his native Gordon. The Baron-Baillie of Greenlaw, William Dickson was the next master though his occupancy was cut short when he sadly died in 1787.

- Education -

*O*ther schoolmasters included William Clinkscale, who was the first
to receive a pension on retirement in 1818, William Hume who's father
David, was a local blacksmith, Andrew Craig, a Fifer who later
emigrated to Australia and finally, his successor John Williamson who
was the last master before the coming of the 20th century.

*I*t is important to note, in the early days of the school, it was not just
a case of teaching the children the basic three 'rs', many were also
taught French, Latin, Greek and mathematics.

*A*t the insistence of the Rev. John Fairbairn, a Free Church School
was opened in 1846 when the first teacher was William Kidd who, after
a few years, emigrated to Tasmania when he was succeeded by
brothers, John and Quentin Kerr. John Connor was next in line in 1870
but he left only four years later to take up a new job and was succeeded
by James Davidson who was the last schoolmaster at the school which
ultimately united with the Parish School.

The old school at Greenlaw – Courtesy of Carol Trotter

*T*here were two 'side schools', one teacher private practices, in the
Burgh. The master in the first was Robert Wilson in 1822, though he
did not have a regular schoolroom and taught the children, first at
Shaw's Lane, then in the Waulk Mill and finally at Todholes. The next

50

such practice was undertaken by James Turnbull who used his own house in Church Street for some time before leaving to work in Stirlingshire combining his duties with those of being a leader in the Scottish Temperance League.

Finally, there was a Dame School with the proprietor being Eppie Currie, a local lady. Dame schools were private affairs where the teaching was always carried out by a woman.

Today, Greenlaw School, as mentioned, still stands in Queens Row and the old Schoolmaster's House still exists at the Health Centre; there are three teachers at the school with the head being Jayne Waite. While some forms of 'higher' education was carried out in the early school, at the teacher's discretion, the children now go to Berwickshire High School in Duns for their secondary education.

In the present day, generally speaking, the children who attend the school, coming from all over the immediate area, including farms, have a much easier time getting to and from the school than in days gone by when children had to walk to school, some up to four miles each way and often in driving wind, rain or snow. They, of course were dressed for the 'occasion' but nothing can really keep the biting cold or rain at bay for long, meaning they invariably arrived at school wet through and freezing. There were radiators waiting to dry wet clothes and they usually had some dry clothes at school to change in to.

There were no dining rooms nor local 'tuck' shops to buy lunch and even if there were, the parents could not afford to give their children money to 'splash out on food' What happened was, the children had their lunch box or as it was known then, their 'leave piece' and a tin bottle was filled with tea which was heated on the radiators in readiness for their 'leave time'. The morning and afternoon breaks were known as leave times and, even if it was blowing a blizzard outside, the children **had** to spend their leave and piece times outside in the freezing cold or soaking wet. It all sounds so cruel but yet it would lead to well adjusted citizens who valued what they had, no matter how little. That form of discipline also gave them a much better outlook on life, the value of money and respect for others, especially their parents and older people.

51

- Education -

*I*n those days, and it is not so long ago and certainly in my lifetime, times were hard but the children soon realised how difficult it was for their parents to cope but cope they did and it made us so much better citizens, ready and more able to cope with adulthood.

**The Old Schoolhouse
now the home of
Greenlaw Health Centre**

- The Churches -
and
- Chapels -

*A*s we have seen, three churches were built in the small town; the old parish kirk which dates from the days of Lindisfarne and has served the parish ever since; the United Presbyterian Church, an association of three congregations, opened in the late 18th century on the High Street near the Old Castle Inn, first as an anti Burgher Church until 1855 when the UP took it over. Later it was home to a Congregational Church until 1920 when it was sold to a garage business. A Secession/Free opened in 1843 in the year of the disruption of the church, and was situated on the opposite side of the High Street but a little to the west. That church was later known as the 'Fairbairn' Church, with good cause as we shall learn in later paragraphs. There were earlier congregations in the town, known as the 'Damside and Easter Meetings'. It is believed, the Free Church congregation also worshipped at a house for many years before the Disruption of 1843 when so many left the Established Church at the behest of Dr. Chalmers as a protest against the continuing power of local lords and landowners over the church and its policies.

*T*he first church in the old parish was at Old Greenlaw, though later, there were also, chapels at Halyburton, Lambden and Rowieston in the company of a private chapel. The old church on the Law has long since disappeared and the site has never been found though a burial ground, thought to be of the old chapel, was found in the 18th century. The church was removed to its present site before 1147 and where its successors have stood every since. We have already mentioned some of the early chaplains but that apart, not much is known of the early kirk.

- The Parish Church -

*I*n 1675, the pre-Reformation kirk was greatly restored to the point it was a virtual rebuild though some were aggrieved it was not a totally new building thus eliminating all from the pre-Reformation days. It is noted with some interest, there does seem some signs on the exterior walls, since the rough cast was removed some years ago, the church was raised in height and certain markers on the walls appear to confirm that; certainly the church was ultimately added to on the west and is now adjoined to the tolbooth clock tower. During that work, up to three floors were found under the existing building holding, what can best be described as a graveyard complete with headstones. Many skeletons were found in the process, buried in an orderly fashion. All that tends, as many believe, to point to the first church, (from the 12th century?) being built in a different position thus the bodies found, were buried in, what was then the graveyard. When the present church had further renovation, more bones were found and the same thing happened twice in the 19th century when heating and drainage systems were being installed. Apart from an early, total rebuild, the only other explanation is, before the Reformation, many of the dead were buried in the church underneath the earthen floors in each successive renewal of the building as happened in many other churches.

The old church stands proudly overlooking the village square and set in its own kirkyard containing many fine stones, symbolic, table and a 15th century cross slab, while some of the more important members of the community had their own burial plots mapped around the graveyard including the Cockburns and the Nisbet family of Lambden. There are many Humes, Fraters and Trotters buried in the kirkyard just as there are so many ministers of the various kirks. A memorial to Robert Gibson JP stands near the entrance to the kirkyard while the benevolent Broomfields are laid to rest in the burial ground including Thomas, one of the most noble members of the Greenlaw community. Of course so many other members of the local society rest in peace in that old kirkyard on the hill and the new cemetery to the east including the great entrepreneur, William S. Happer who gave so much to the community, along with his parents, and many other members of his family.

On reaching the tower, the first notable structure is the shaft of the original Greenlaw (mercat) Cross, a reminder of the prominent days of yesteryear. The shaft stands alongside the tower which still contains its original, grim iron grill gate and windows. Along side the old Cross are some delightful, ancient stones including one of the noble Humes.

- Greenlaw -

Greenlaw Kirk from the north-east side of the old kirkyard

    *T*he kirk is built of random rubblestone with ashlar dressings. There are no less than nine windows gracing the south elevation, two on the west, one on the east and four on the north. Apart from the great 78 feet tall tolbooth tower, there is another tower like structure, a turnpike stairway, added at the east of the main tower. The steeply sloping roof is covered in grey slate and the gables are endowed with period crow steps. With the addition of the north aisle in 1855, the building was transformed from a rectangle to 'T' shape.

    *T*he interior is entered by the south-west entrance though there are no less than four entrances to the building. We enter below the west gallery, one of three such galleries in the kirk, the others to the north and east. Sections of pews face the pulpit on the south wall from east, west and north, all with central aisles. The great windows on the south wall have venetian blinds, an excellent idea considering the light which showers in on fine days, allowing the congregation to see their minister. It is interesting, seeing the depth of the recesses at the windows, allowing a glimpse of the thickness of the walls, more than three feet thick, giving more evidence of the antiquity of the lower sections of the building. A grouping of single seats populate the area to the west of the pulpit and are used by the church choir facing, directly opposite, one of the great organs of the Borders. In the north aisle, in more recent times, work has been carried out, converting the old boiler house in to a kitchen and disabled friendly toilet. The communion area is reached by three steps and, apart from the pulpit, there is the communion table, minister's chair and an elders' pew. The pulpit is reached by winding stairs with balustrade and above, high on the south wall, is a beautiful hand made cross, made by a Polish member of the community, gifted to the kirk and dedicated to the memory of Matthew Leitch. (1880-1966) Behind the pulpit, is a beautifully carved and arcaded, columned screen.

The West Gallery and the great organ to the right

*F*ixed to the walls to the east are three pointed screens containing the Beatitudes, the Lord's Prayer and the 23rd Psalm. Near the organ there is a thought provoking scroll providing a Roll of Honour naming all the young men of the parish who went off to fight in the Great War and, almost immediately in front and below is a fine octagonal, timber font.

*T*he vestry, on the north, is full of memories, old and new photographs of ministers and Kirk Sessions through the ages grace the walls, and another of HRH Princess Margaret, who attended a service in 1952 while she was staying at Marchmont. Another old frame contains a painting of the old county building with the church, tolbooth and courthouse in the background.

*I*t is a wonderful old church, well worthy of being, at one stage, the church of the most important town and parish in the county of Berwick. It still dominates, as it always has done, tall and proud above the town square. The minister is Rev. Thomas Nicholson who has been serving the communities of Berwickshire since 1995; Greenlaw Church is linked with Gordon, linked with Westruther, linked with Legerwood. Mrs. Carol Trotter is the latest of a very long line of Session clerks at the Kirk.

*O*n the 5th April, 2015, no less a day than Easter Sunday, the local churches were honoured with the visit of the Moderator of the General Assembly of the Church of Scotland, the Right Reverend John Chalmers at Westruther Kirk.

A selection of gravestones in the Kirkyard

- Churches -

The Cockburn Mausoleum

Fenced off for safety reasons and is classified 'A Building at Risk'

The Nisbet of Lambden Burial Aisle

Greenlaw Cemetery

courtesy of Walter Baxter

- Greenlaw -

*T*he first known preacher at the church after the Reformation in 1560, was the 'reader', Charles Home, who was almost certainly a priest of the old faith and who also held the chaplaincy at Halyburton. The first known, fully ordained minister? David Hume in 1603.

List of known ministers and their year of taking charge

1567....Charles Home*   1569.....John Affleck*   1573....Robert French*   1590....William Fraser* 1603.....David Hume
1638.....Charles Spence   1645....Robert Hume   1674.....John Home
1693.....Archibald Borthuik   1707.....David Brown, joint minister for a time with Archibald Borthuik   1711.....James Gilliland
1725.....Thomas Turnbull   1734.....John Hume
1778.....William Simpson   1799.....John Stewart   1804.....James Luke
1821.....Abraham Hume   1844.....John Walker   1882.....Arthur Graham   1886.....Hugh MacCulloch   1916.....Thomas Thomson
1944.....George Johnston 1953.....Alexander Lawson
1962.....George Chalmers 1968.....Frederich Levison
1978.....Ian Paterson   1985.....Robert Higham
1991-94.....Ian Wotherspoon   1995-present.....Thomas Nicholson

*Almost certainly readers

Original Secession and Free Church

*T*here is evidence there have been dissenting parishioners and churchmen at Greenlaw since the late 18th century but, in the case of the Original Secession Church or the Auld Licht as it became known, the first mention arrives in 1807 when the *Damside Meeting* was formed by Alexander Ritchie of Rumbleton and the Stobie brothers, Thomas and William who had a tailors' business in Greenlaw. They were all members of the Stichill Burgher Church but when a new minister was appointed, they all disagreed with the new preacher's form of service and decided to open their own meeting place in a building near the

Waulk Mill. They were served with visiting ministers for a while before Rev. John Inglis was called to the charge but more trouble was brewing and, once again, the Stobies were on their way. This time they held meetings in their own home and continued as 'temporary ministers' until they died.

*M*r. Inglis was a busy man and had to carry out the good work on his own, often taking service seven days a week. In time his health deteriorated and he died in 1832. A new minister, James Young was called but in 1839, most of the congregation left and joined the Parish Kirk. Mr. Young carried on for a while before resigning, leaving the way for John Fairbairn, who was working in Canada, to be called to the charge and, in so many ways, changed the course of local history. John Fairbairn was a local man, growing up as he did, at Halyburton, and attended the local parish school with his older brother, Patrick, of whom we shall hear more of in later pages. Though his wife's health was a key factor in his returning to Scotland, it could not have been better timed since John was more of the secessionist variety of minister than the ministers of the established national kirk.

*I*n 1843, barely a year after Mr. Fairbairn's return, a huge schism occurred within the kirk and many congregations broke away from the Church of Scotland to form the Free Church. There were many reasons for the break but, it would appear, the principal cause was the continuing *Right of Patronage,* where the local lord, who was the principal heritor of the church, had the ability to choose who the minister should be and, of course, send him packing when the good laird saw fit. This was an unpalatable situation for many, thus the split.

*J*ohn Fairbairn oversaw the building of a fine new church and a Free Kirk School... education was key to his beliefs and he ensured there was choice for the local children; his school still stands as the Fairbairn Hall in the village. His church has sadly, long since, departed the scene though many of the local people still remember the building fondly and still refer to it as the *Fairbairn Kirk.*

The Fairbairn Kirk dominates the skyline in a view from the Parish Church Tower
Courtesy of Carol Trotter

*T*he grand building dominated the skyline on West High Street and the ground it occupied still lies empty covered with grass and a pathway adjacent to Fairbairn Court which itself occupies the site of a garage and petrol station. The gateway in to the grounds still exists as a form of memorial to the church with the most inspiring conical steeple. It was built of local stone in the form of a rectangle with the longer east and west walls held together by great buttresses. Each side contained four tall, pointed windows reaching high towards the sloping, slated roof. The north gable was home to a magnificent pointed window reaching towards the heavens while the south, entrance elevation, was endowed with a sublime pointed and layered archway surrounding the doorway with pointed windows on either side. The tower, which graced the entrance gable contained two smaller windows with one each on the east and west elevations. All the windows, of the most subtly stained glass, were heavenly treasures and works of the highest order.

*T*he old church was later used for storage by an antique firm before the end came. In the present day, such a wonderful building would never have been allowed to be destroyed, as it was, and lost forever.

John Fairbairn was granted an assistant in 1875 in the shape of the Reverend Alexander Cameron who later assumed full ministry until his retirement in 1902. It took nearly two years to find another minister but the post was filled in 1904 by Rev. Hugh Harper who served through the 1st World War before retiring in 1925 and being replaced by George Calvert in who's ministry, the church rejoined the established kirk in 1929. George moved on in 1931 making way for Rev. Ewan Cameron who served for ten years before being replaced by Alexander Houston in 1941, and served until the end of World War Two in 1945. Robert Porter was his successor, a man who served the congregation until 1949; the last minister at the church, before it closed in the earlier part of the 1950s, was William G. Jeffrey. (see more of Rev. Fairbairn in 'notable people'

Secession, General Associate, United Presbyterian, Congregational

Situated on the south of the High Street at the Square, this congregation was originally known as the *Easter Meeting* which was a part of the Antiburgher section of the United Secession Church which later joined the General Associate Synod which, in turn, united with the Relief Church forming the United Presbyterian Church before spending its final days as part of the Congregational Church. Sounds complicated but throughout the 19th and well in to the 20th century, the Presbyterian denomination had several 'offshoots' where very small differences in their way of worship caused many schisms throughout the centuries leading up to and including the 20th century.

The congregation is first mentioned in 1782 but is thought to be a few years older. At first they held their services in a a barn at Broomhill Farm before, in 1791, they purchased two, two storey houses, one of which was an inn, in East High Street, which were converted and co-joined to act as their place of worship. Those buildings were purchased for the princely sum of £115 by John Purves of Purves Hall, one of the elders. The church was very much of its time with thatched roof and earthen floor covered in mud on wet days. That continued for some time, during which the building was constantly being upgraded before, in 1885, the building we still see, was erected.

A list of the early ministers is available including the first, John McVitie, who was called in 1785 and who walked all the way from his home in Amisfield in Dumfriesshire to take up his charge. As it happened, his walk was made worthwhile when a grand party was laid on for him in the Castle Inn by the landlady, Martha Brown. Martha, one of the local 'worthies', made no mistakes however and charged £2 a ticket for the minister's welcoming bash (£2 was a rather large amount of money in those far off days) however it all went well and the good minister was given a right royal welcome. Martha was a legend in her time and was even mentioned in Walter Scott's novel, *Waverley.* Mr McVitie died in 1785 at the young age of 35 and was interred in Greenlaw Kirkyard. It was two years later, in 1787, before a new minister, John Parker, joined the congregation. Mr. Parker left his post in 1807 and was later noted to have published two volumes of his work, *Parker's Letters.* The next minister, David Inglis, was appointed after his interview in the town's Crown Inn. Mr Inglis helped set up the Bible Society in Greenlaw in 1815 and was also responsible for establishing the first Sunday School in the town which was open to all the children of Greenlaw no matter which church they had connection with.

The Congregational Church as it is today

- Churches -

*R*obert Monteath was the next to be given the charge when he
arrived in !841 to be assistant to Mr Inglis and, in 1842, on the death of
Mr Inglis, became minister in his own right. Mr Monteath left Greenlaw
in 1854 to take up a charge in Canada and was succeeded by Rev. John
Milne. Peter Wilson was next to take the post in 1879 but resigned in
1895 to be followed by James Padkin who later resigned in 1903 to take
up a new challenge in Paisley.

*T*he Rev. G. B. Piercy is the first known minister when the church
moved over to the Congregational movement and he served from 1909
until 1919. He then moved to Ayr where he conducted service until
1921 when he died at the age of 39 years and was returned to Greenlaw,
a place he loved, for burial. Though his ministry was during the dates
mentioned, it is noted he served as a lieutenant in the armed forces
during the Great War of 1914-1918 and ultimately died of wounds
received during that war.

- Lambden Chapel -

*A*part from the church at Old Greenlaw, Lambden Chapel or more
correctly Lambden Church, was perhaps, the first church in the parish
having been founded sometime, at the earliest, 1073AD and the latest,
1140AD. The reason behind those dates is the names of all concerned,
for instance, Earl Cospatric being granted the lands, his son, also
Cospatric inheriting the lands, the granting of the right to build or
probably to enlarge a church, to Sir Walter de Strivelyn on the premise
it was dedicated to Earl Cospatric and his family for all time, and
finally, the rights of the de Strivelyn (Stirling) family to grant the
church and lands to the new abbey at Kelso, which was founded in 1128
by King David I. The Royal Commission on Ancient buildings is quite
unclear on the Lambden foundation, citing "before the end of the 11th
century" and "before 1147". Whatever the date, the church, dedicated to
St. Mary, in the *Dene of the lambs* 'punched above its weight'

*T*he kirk, which formed the heart of a sizeable village, was indeed
an important foundation both before and after its being granted to the

mother church at Greenlaw. Evidence of that is witnessed in the number of important men of Lambden and so many charters made in the name of church, village and, of course, noble men who lived and worked there.

Quite apart from Cospatric and Walter de Strivelyn, we know of Walter's son John de Lambden, the first to adopt the name of the lands, then Henry de Lambden who became Abbot of Kelso under some dubious circumstances. He was chancellor to the abbot when he made a pilgrimage to Rome where he met the pope, Alexander IV. He then returned to Kelso with a Papal letter to the Abbot of Kelso, Patrick, essentially saying his, Patrick's, services were no longer required and his chancellor, Henry, was now the new abbot at the abbey. When Henry de Lambden died, it is thought the monks rejoiced, since they had been deeply suspicious of his motives which led to him being installed to the abbacy in the first place.

Others included, Walter de Lambden, son of John, William who was the church's chaplain in 1160, Robert of Lambden who was a qualified notary in 1250, Roland who was master of the village around the same time, 1200AD, as we hear of another chaplain, Nigel.

Though a village church which appeared in the *Ancient Taxatio*, Lambden was a dependency of Greenlaw, and was thus known as a chapel, with its own chaplain and, from time to time, visitations of ordained brothers from Kelso Abbey. All forms of services were carried out except on the great Feast Days when the people of Lambden had to make the journey north for worship at Greenlaw Parish Church. Lambden Chapel continued beyond the Reformation of 1560 though sections were rebuilt after the Earl of Hertford's destructive visit in 1545. Sadly the small church of St. Mary is thought to have closed forever before the end of the 16th century.

The great annual Lambden Fair however, continued in to the 19th century, and it was a busy and important fair at that. Buying, selling and the hiring of new 'hands' for the nearby farms were carried out before the workers 'bounties' were spent in a local 'tippling house' The fair was always opened in a very orderly and structured fashion beginning with local dignitaries, dressed formally, marching in to the village to the beat of drums. The laird led the parade, marching to the clash of steel to stone as he pounded his spear to the ground. That spear of office is still kept in Lambden House, slightly to the north of the site of the old village which is now occupied by a farm. The chapel, which possessed a gruesome pair of restraining jougs, and its graveyard were situated on the eastern edge of the present farm buildings at Grid Reference NT7448 4298, a few kilometres to the south-east of Greenlaw.

- Halyburton Chapel -

*A*round three miles north-west of Greenlaw, stands the old farm of Haliburton, reached from the Edinburgh Road near to the Wester Bridge. Haliburton is an ancient name in the area, and where a small settlement grew from, possibly, the late 11th century when Cospatric granted lands to Triute, the leader of the family who ultimately became known as the Haliburtons, a family who would stretch far and wide, all across the world, with a great deal of dignity and piety. The site of the old chapel is believed to be at Grid Ref. NT6733 4852 just a few yards to the south of the farm houses on the opposite side of the road.

*T*he name Halyburton or Haliburton may be from one of two old names from south of the Border, Barton or Burton. The Anglo-Saxon name, Barton emanating from barley and tun meaning a settlement, perhaps a farm settlement where barley is grown or, more likely, Burton, being derived from Old English as '*Settlement by the fort*" Therefore, it is likely, the first proprietors of the lands, built some kind of fortifications. The prefix of 'Haly or Holy' appears to have been added when a church or chapel was built thus forming the name we now know and the family who first lived there.

*I*t is possible Triute built the first church there before he passed the lands to his son, David who, in turn, granted the church and land in to the hands of the Tironesian monks of Kelso. David's, sons, Walter and Henri de Halyburton made further grants to the abbey before his grandson Phillipe's wife, Alicia, swore fealty to Edward I at Berwick in

1296. Other members of the 13th century Halyburtons were, Adam, William and another Walter, all designated 'de Halyburton'.

*T*he church, like that at Lambden, was rated in the *Ancient Taxatio* being valued at 40 merks, and again like its sister chapel 'down the road' was given over as a dependant chapel of the Mother Kirk at Greenlaw when Greenlaw was granted to Kelso Abbey in 1147. Chaplains were generally provided by the abbey but it is more than possible, Charles Hume was the last Roman Catholic priest at Haliburton before the Reformation as we have already seen. He was, in the aftermath of the Scottish religious revolution, the first reader at Hume Kirk and, probably, at Greenlaw. Many of the Catholic clergy did act as readers and some even studied and were ordained in to the new national Church of Scotland. Another chaplain at Halyburton was appointed and presented to the chapel in 1319 by Edward II, during one of his forays north of the Border.

*T*he chapel was dedicated to St. Mary and, while it was largely destroyed by the forces of Edward Seymour, Earl of Hertford, in 1545, it was still 'operating' for a short time after the Reformation with the aforementioned Charles Hume dividing his time there, with the other churches in the area. Some of the broken stones from the old church were said to have been used in the building of the farmstead long after the small village disappeared. If that is the case, then just a little of the ancient history, of an ancient church, village and family, still lives in the place of its birth.

- Rowiestone Chapel -

*T*he origins of this chapel are enshrouded in mystery and nothing has been seen of it since the mid 19th century in the midst of a great copse of ancient trees. It was situated at Grid Ref. NT7456 4558 and is near Angelrow Farm off the A697 Greenlaw to Coldstream road. The view on the opposite side of the road and looking away from Angelrow, is a large density of trees which are only a couple of hundred yards away. In the midst of the trees is a very deep pond which was dug out on the site of the chapel and its graveyard. Nothing at all of the chapel or kirkyard can now be seen, though, in the middle of the 19th century, gravestones and piles of great boulders were reported on the site.

The chapel was never truly in the dependency of Greenlaw, but, while it was more in the realm of Melrose Abbey, it has always been associated with Auld Grinlae.

- Roland de Greenlaw's private chapel -

It is not entirely clear what family Roland was related to, was it the original family of Old Greenlaw, which I suspect it was, or was he a member of the Cospatric family? Whatever the case, he requested the abbot at Kelso to allow him build a private chapel within his enclosed court. Whether that court was at Greenlaw Castle or in a fortified house on the Law, we may never know, it is all so vague. Having considered Roland's request, the abbot, Osbert, and his monks, decided he, Roland, could erect his chapel for his household and men at arms use but all must attend Greenlaw Church on the Sabbath. Any contributions Roland or his followers made, were all to be given to the Mother Church. In return, the abbot would allow his chaplain to visit the private chapel on three days every week but not on a Sunday.

- Notable People -

Who is a notable person? Is it one who has achieved much success in their own vocation or given either monetary or truly personal assistance to the community at large or simply have association with the town? Yes, of course, all of those are the case but it can also apply to those who have not quite reached the heights of benevolence, though they have soared high in the annals of the region even for notoriety, so notorious to be given the title 'noteworthy' albeit for the wrong reasons. There are so many from both sides of the coin. People like the English Kings, Edward I, II and III who all laid waste to the region were 'notable' as was Henry VIII's brother-in-law, Edward Seymour, the Earl of Hertford who later went on to be Protector of England as the Duke of Somerset, but not of the wanted variety and would never appear on our Christmas Card list. Centuries before of course, Old Greenlaw was the subject of countless invasions as we have already seen, from the Romans, the Angles, Saxons and Vikings who could claim to being 'noteworthy' but let us begin with three members of the Royal Family who visited in more recent times, all whom we have already mentioned.

Princess Margaret visited the church before her sister, Queen Elizabeth II visited the town in 1984 while her son, Charles, Duke of Rothesay, did his 'turn' in opening the Town Hall. All of those occasions were supported by the local populace who turned out in droves, an audience which was swelled by hundreds of well wishers from all across the region and beyond.

Many men of Marchmont and Purves Hall did so much for the people of Greenlaw but perhaps the man who did most was Sir William Purves-Hume-Campbell the 6th Baronet. He was born in 1767 at Marchmont, the son of Sir Alexander Purves, 5th Baronet. He was a brilliant academic but it was not until he ascended to the Baronetcy, his true colours unravelled, he most certainly was a man of the people. He provided so much, a poor fund, literally created work for returning soldiers of the Napoleonic Wars, in an effort to prevent starvation of young families in Greenlaw, gave endowments to help with the upkeep of the church, financed the first fresh water system in the town in 1829 and formed a steel company to build great bunkers which the good lord filled with coal for the people. The coal was not free but was estimated to be less than a quarter of the cost of buying it from the coal merchants thus saving the poor a little more money.

Perhaps, though, he is best remembered as the man who financed the building of the new County Hall from 1828 until 1831 when it was completed. As we have seen, the hall cost some £6,500 which would equate to a quite astonishing sum in the present day. The great man died only two years later, in 1833, at Marchmont having lived his life, not only as an aristocrat but indeed, as a friend and true servant of his people. He is, most surely, one of Greenlaw's greatest sons both in life and death when more money and benefits were bequeathed to the poor of the parish.

Robert Boyne Home was the last of that male line born at Greenlaw Castle, the son of William Home and Anne Purves who moved to their new estate at Sharplaw shortly after their son's birth in 1713. Robert went on to qualify as a surgeon before moving his practice to Kingston upon Hull where he was a much respected doctor particularly with his patients who came to idolise him. His son, Sir Everard Home scaled the heights of medicine and surgery becoming the King's Sergeant-Surgeon in 1808 before being appointed Surgeon-General at Chelsea Hospital. Everard's sister Anne Home, married surgeon, John Hunter before becoming famous in her own right as a poet and of writing the English words to the music of Joseph Hayden.

Another man of note and such a wonderfully benevolent man he was, to church, school and people, was Thomas Broomfield. He was always willing to help during his lifetime but his last wish was to leave a large portion of his money to the church, the school and the poor of the town; what else was left over after his wife died, was also to be added to his benevolent fund. Sadly that most generous bequest became just a little messy and took over a century after his death to fully implement in full.

In his will, he mentioned all the local lords and dignitaries, asking them to ensure his bequest was distributed properly and in the manner he requested, like, for instance, a new bell for the church, to build a new bridge at Wester Row, funds for the poor and needy and for the education of the children. John Craw, a local man, was appointed executor and things went along nicely to begin with. The bridge was built and 'ane guid belle' was installed at the kirk but problems arose after Mr. Broomfield's wife died. Mr Craw felt all had been done but it would appear, he wished to keep some of the money, he even claimed the Crown had awarded the estate to him since it was said to be an 'Estate of Bastardy'. Eventually, court case after case came and went until it was finally decided, some of the local barons should look after the Broomfield money but again problems arose. Mr Broomfield's final will and testament was not fully enacted until 1748. Had it not been for the Purves Baronets, the Broomfield bequest may never have been fully implemented. As part of the Purves intervention in the estate, they also undertook to keep the church bell mechanism in good working but in 1888, the bell from Marchmont was used as a replacement for the old Broomfield Bell at the same time as a clock was installed as part of Queen Victoria's Jubilee celebrations.

In more modern times, several families have been of great benefit to the local economy. The Frater family of the stone masonry, steel and building company were said to treat their employees with the greatest respect and were known to help out in times of need. The same applied to the joinery and coffin making company owned by the local Darling company. That was also the case of the Trotters and Happers, other old families of Greenlaw, indeed the Happer name is guaranteed to live on in to posterity as we have already witnessed.

Robert Young, a man who could 'turn his hand' to any job, was another who did so much for the town. It was he who gathered the group to help him create the first electricity system; he was also said to have helped make improvements to the water system, repairing the Town Clock, in fact if anything out of the ordinary which was requiring repair, it was a case of sending for Mr. Young. He too, was responsible for leaving us his own observations of Greenlaw which complimented the history of the town which was written by Robert Gibson in the early 20th Century. Mr. Young's story was left via an audio tape but was put to paper in the fine publication, *The Road to Grinlae,* in 1996 by his son, Russell Young. Robert Gibson's book, *An Old Berwickshire town, A History of the Town and Parish of Greenlaw from the earliest times to the present day* was edited by his son, Thomas Gibson, in 1905. Therefore Robert Young and Robert Gibson must surely be considered most notable men of the their beloved home, Greenlaw and thanks to their sons, their words will live forever.

The Happer family are indeed one of the best known families in the parish and, in their time...and beyond, have left their mark. The Happers were predominately a family tailor business but in time bought other businesses in the town including Stoddarts Stores. George purchased Greenlaw Mill and farm lands before renting lands back to farmers for grazing. In time the Greenlaw Games, thanks to Mr. Happer, were being enacted on the haugh lands on the right bank of the Blackadder. On his death, the estate came to his son William S. who further developed the family business and sold off much of the farmlands but retained the field south of the river. William died in 1970 when the estate passed to his son, Alex who, with his sister Mrs. Ann Trotter, decided to gift the lands to the community in 1978 when a beautiful cairn was erected. There was a further act of unveiling in 1993 when the woodlands were officially opened by Mrs Trotter. The rest is of course, is history but it is still worth mentioning again, since the woodlands and park are in constant use thanks to those acts of benevolence,

William S. Happer
Courtesy of Carol Trotter

such a wonderful gift to the people of Greenlaw, has become living history. That lovely scene to the east of the village will live long and provide so much relaxation and fun for many generations to come. The Community Council now care for the park, they organised the tree planting and it is they, with help, who keep it up to scratch, spick and span. In fact the latest clean up of the woodlands took place as recently as March, 2015. Now the council members are looking to install benches for the use of walkers especially those with older legs...like me. Everyone of those councillors and their helpers, are indeed notable people of today.

Many of the church ministers served a very large proportion of their lives at Greenlaw while some died during their ministry including James Luke, who was killed in a riding accident. All of those men are notable in their own right for the work they have done, and still do within the community.

*E*very minister, including the pre-Refomation parsons and chaplains, gave so much to the town and parish. Theirs is not simply to preach on a Sunday morning, theirs is to care for and offer solace to all, at all times, whether they be practising Christians or not. To baptise the new born baby, to help induct children and adults in to God's Church and guide them in the path of goodness. They then join the ones they baptised all those years earlier, in to Holy Matrimony and later baptise their children too and, finally, they pray for their souls in death and help them reach even closer to the Lord. They also visit their flock whether at home or in hospital when they are sick and in need, without their guiding hands, the world would a much poorer place. That situation applies to all preachers of all congregations of all denominations at all times, all men of note.

*O*ne minister of Greenlaw who become a legendary figure, with housing, the long gone church on West High Street and the church hall, all named in his honour was, of course, John Fairbairn, one of the best loved and best known of all the parish residents and he was indeed a local man, born at Halyburton in 1808 and educated at Greenlaw School. John was a secessionist and a minister of that church having been ordained at Cupar in Fife before emigrating to Canada where he spread the good word for nine years before being called to his native Greenlaw just before the Disruption of 1843. He was responsible for the building and opening of the Free Church School in 1846 and devoted much of his time to help teach the children in his charge.

*J*ohn married twice, his first wife, Mary Wilson, mother of his son, died young before later marrying Agnes Turnbull of Eyemouth: His son later emigrated to Queensland, Australia with his family. John died at Dunbar in East Lothian in 1895 and was returned to his beloved Greenlaw for burial where he lies at peace, his work complete.

*S*ome would say, John is Greenlaw's son of sons, a proverbial giant of a man. His name will indeed live on forever, not only in the hall and the homes on West High Street named in his honour but also in the stories, legends and history of the town.

*J*ohn was of a family of well educated men including his brother, Patrick and his cousins, James Fairbairn of Bedshiel and Dr. John Purves of Purves Hall. James was a Free Church minister at Newhaven at Edinburgh while John was a doctor of note at Edinburgh but it was his brother Patrick who attained the greatest fame.

*P*atrick Fairbairn, like his younger brother, John, was educated at Greenlaw Parochial School and Edinburgh University before going on to be a teacher on Orkney. He was then given the charge of North Ronaldsay Church where he spent six years before moving on to Glasgow to take the charge at Bridgeton. He was later minister at Saltoun in East Lothian before, in 1843, at the Disruption, he joined the newly formed Free Church where his life would change forever.

*T*en years later, in 1853, he was appointed Professor of Theology at Aberdeen before becoming Professor and Principal of the Free Church College in Glasgow where he remained for the rest of his life.

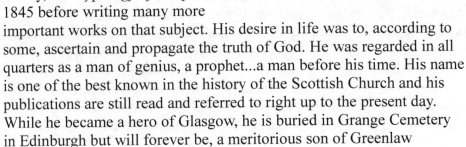

Patrick Fairbairn
by John Maclehose
(Wikipedia see acknowledgements)

*H*e wrote what was one of the most important theological publications of its day, *The Typology of Scripture* in 1845 before writing many more important works on that subject. His desire in life was to, according to some, ascertain and propagate the truth of God. He was regarded in all quarters as a man of genius, a prophet...a man before his time. His name is one of the best known in the history of the Scottish Church and his publications are still read and referred to right up to the present day. While he became a hero of Glasgow, he is buried in Grange Cemetery in Edinburgh but will forever be, a meritorious son of Greenlaw

- Greenlaw -

*P*atrick Christie, the first schoolmaster gave up much of his salary to buy books for his pupils and he must surely be considered as one of the town's most notable and benevolent men. Many of his counterparts, all of whom were responsible for the early education of the town's notables were as generous in both time and gifts. Doctors too made their mark in the town but none more so than Patrick Kynoch who arrived in the practice at the tender age of 21 and served his patients faithfully for 29 years before he died in 1893 aged only 50 years old, and was interred in the kirkyard.

*I*t is sad there are so few women mentioned but that was more a sign of the times when women were 'to be seen and not heard'. During the era in which they lived, they were treated more as servants and the bearers of the children and of course, they were too pre-occupied in raising their bairns. The wives of the landed gentry were a different case and many of them did make contributions. On the other hand, women in those days, were not obligated to go and fight in wars as their husbands did, they had to stay at home to take care of the children and we all know that the most notable person in every child's life is their mother. Sadly, some of those mothers and children were never to see their husbands or fathers again which takes us to the most notable of all men, the heroes who died for us all in an effort to ensure our lives and lands would be safe for future generations. Here follows the full list of men who died for us. Their names appear on the War Memorial in front of the Mercat Cross and the County Hall, the full list is on the following page, *Lest we Forget.*

War Memorial - The Great War 1914 -18

Thomas Alder – King's Own Scottish Borderers
John Anderson – Dublin Royal Fusiliers
Adam Anderson – King's Own Scottish Borderers
Robert Baxter – King's Own Scottish Borderers
John Buckham – King's Own Scottish Borderers
William Cockburn – Royal Highlanders, The Black Watch
James Cockburn – King's Own Scottish Borderers
Robert Clapham – King's Own Scottish Borderers
Mathew Clapham – King's Own Scottish Borderers
William D. Clark – Scottish Rifles
John Douglas DCM – King's Own Scottish Borderers
Robert Douglas – King's Own Scottish Borderers
James Darling – Canadians
William Henry – King's Own Scottish Borderers
Robert Happer – Canadians
William Hall – Scottish Rifles
Thomas Mather – Highland Light Infantry
John Mallen – Scots Guards
Alexander Murray – King's Own Scottish Borderers
William Moffat – King's Own Scottish Borderers
Fred Routledge – Scottish Horse
William Redpath – Royal Scots
Robert Robertson – King's Own Scottish Borderers
James Speedy – Royal Highlanders, The Black Watch
Daniel Stuart – Royal Scots
George Somerville – Royal Navy
William Scott – King's Own Scottish Borderers
George C. Scott – Highland Light Infantry
Albert Trotter – Argyll and Sutherland Highlanders
Robert P. Thomson – Rifle Brigade
Robert Walker – King's Own Scottish Borderers
Robert Whitehead – King's Own Scottish Borderers
George Wright – Royal Highlanders, The Black Watch
*Andrew C. Burns - 3rd Scottish Border Battalion, Home Guard

- War Memorial -

W. Jenkinson – Seaforth Highlanders
George B. Piercy – Royal Scots

Not on memorial but buried in Greenlaw Kirkyard

World War Two 1939-45

Adam G. Balmer – Merchant Navy
Andrew Burns – Home Guard
George Richardson – Fleet Air Arm
William Trotter – Royal Air Force

We all owe those brave men and boys who died for us, a great deal of gratitude and, while their efforts may not have prevented future conflicts, their sacrifice did lessen the danger for their loved ones left behind. In all our eyes, every one of them, without doubt, are heroes.

**Greenlaw War Memorial
with the Mercat Cross and County Hall in the background**

- Notable People -

*O*f course, all the aforementioned people are now written into the history and folklore of the Parish but as time moves on, more people arrive on the scene helping the community in so many ways. Some have formed groups and clubs to help make life a little more interesting and enjoyable for the community at large while others take the extra step to enhance what the town already has. The teaching of children still goes on, doctors and nurses still care for us as does the minister, Reverend Tom Nicholson, who has served his flock faithfully and diligently for 20 years, 20 years of wholesome devotion to the people of Greenlaw and the nearby parishes of Westruther, Gordon and Legerwood.

A group of people keep the woodlands clean and tidy and have made plans to raise money to install benches along the way in an effort to make things a little easier. Some of that group help keep the village clean and one has even painted benches in his efforts to keep his beloved Greenlaw looking bright and breezy. Those are all noble acts of proud, notable people, helping make their town more acceptable and pleasing for others within the community, and visitors.

*T*hen there are people who hang on to old photographs which will help the present and future generations to better understand earlier days in the ancient county town of Berwickshire, Carol Trotter, a Community Councillor and Kirk Session Clerk falls in to that category and. her photos of the old town have helped me much more than words can say. Her involvement in helping maintain awareness of Greenlaw's proud past will live long in to the future. Others too, like Doug Smith, who has lived in Greenlaw all his life, knows more about the town than anyone and has helped me, like Carol, immensely, He has the history of Greenlaw in his head and I hope his help with this humble rendering will keep the old story going for future generations. In his younger days, Doug was asked if he cared to 'wind' up the town clock, a job which had to be done every week of the year. Doug was interested in the position but when he was offered the princely sum of £12 a year, it was too good to turn down. Of course, one of the benefits was, the view from the top of the tower, Doug could see everything which was going on all around, including the gravedigger, William aka Wull Watson.

- Greenlaw -

Wull was indeed a character who doubled up as the street sweeper when not preparing graves. In time he felt he needed an apprentice and his nephew, Dan Horsburgh (only 14 years old) came to live at Greenlaw to be Uncle Wull's apprentice. Wull had many rituals and one of those was to greet a funeral cortege at the gates of the cemetery and lead the way to the grave. One day when a burial was due, a deluge of rain arrived causing the newly dug grave to fill with water. Wull instructed Dan, "Get down there son and pail out as if your life depended on it!" Young Dan was busy emptying out the water when Wull disappeared to meet the grieving family. As the funeral party neared the grave, Dan was still busy with the bucket. Suddenly Wull called out to Dan, "You better hurry up son, the new tenant is arriving" We can only imagine what the grieving family felt. Apart from digging graves and sweeping streets, Wull, or, in his official role, William, was the town piper for many years and a member of the Kirk Session. Like the afore mentioned Martha Brown, Wull is notable as another of the town's enduring list of colourful 'worthies'. Those are the people of yesteryear and today, and there are many others, whom I consider 'notable' for the right reasons in a world which is somehow losing its way in the modern age. They follow faithfully in the paths of those who have long since departed, some of them poor, some of them wealthy noblemen who lived in the 'big house' up the road so, before we finally say our goodbyes to ancient Greenlaw, let's take a peek in to where some of those of the more noble variety lived.

- Where the Lairds lived - Purves Hall -

*T*he name Purves or Purvis is said to derive from the people who acquired goods for the early kings in Scotland, *the purveyors* but perhaps that is a bit simplistic. Many believe the family originated in Normandy but that is quite unsubstantiated though there is mention of the name from medieval times when men like William de Purveys made a grant of land to Melrose Abbey in 1214 and Alan Purvays bore witness to a charter of Patrick, Earl of March in 1318. Other known

Purves Hall

members of the family were Andrew Purves who was witness to a charter in 1438 but the most interesting, in the context of Berwickshire was Thomas Purves who received a charter of lands from the Duke of Albany in 1427. Whether the lands were of what became known as Purves Hall is not clear but there is every reason to believe, Thomas was the first known of the family who ultimately made contribution to the Parish of Greenlaw. The great house, Purves Hall is thought to have been built in the later part of the 16th century and though it was fortified, it would not see too much 'action' since the days of the *Wars of the Rough Wooing* of the middle of the 16th century had come and gone with a form of peace reigning over the Kingdoms of Scotland and England.

*P*urves Hall was a rectangular building of a mix of two and three storeys described as having 3 x 2 bays meaning there were three windows at each level on the longest section and two windows on each floor of the 'gables'. It was constructed of random whinstone rubble and sandstone with cream, ashlar dressings. The windows each contained 12 panes within timber sash and case, making for a bright interior which, by any standards of the day was unusual. That was the house in which the family lived, conducted their business, raised their families and, ultimately, died; that is until their move to Marchmont in 19th century.

*I*n 1790, a new 'wing' was added to the rear of the house and, interestingly, that is the section which is still occupied as a private home since the original tower house was allowed to crumble after the family's departure to the 'Big House of the Humes'. Interestingly, a Colonel John Hume Purves was living in the house in 1866.

*T*he building itself is very much a relic of the 17th/18th century style large house. It contains the most supreme fireplaces, of differing styles but one, similar to the great fireplace at the visitor centre at Queen Mary's House in Jedburgh, 'steals the show'. That great arched fireplace in the dining room would once be used to cook the meals and it is not difficult to imagine, the cook hanging the pots and pans over the burning embers while preparing the laird's and his guests' suppers. Before they partook of their food and wine they would marvel at the carved and lavishly adorned ceilings of Renaissance tempera painted works so akin to period houses of the day, across the whole of Scotland some of which I have had the great pleasure in witnessing.

The large house, still containing sections of the original edifice, acts as a time honoured peep in to the past, exhibiting the glorious workmanship of the day, which only the rich and powerful could afford.

Another house was built at Purves Hall, slightly, to the south of the old building, and that house too contains a section of the original tower-house. The 'new' house was built in the 19th century but all I can say is, it really is a fine country house which shares an ancient walled garden with the older house next door. The new house though was never, in itself, a known domain of the principal Purves family.

Both houses are situated just a few kilometres south-east of Greenlaw near Eccles Tofts farm and is reached via a minor road off the A697 Greenlaw to Coldstream road. They both retain the name, Purves Hall only differentiated by the words tower and house. It is unusual to find two such fine houses, of the same name in the same estate.

The first Purves we know, with connection to Purves Hall, is the man who built the great tower-house after being created the 1st Baronet in 1665 was Sir William. His son, Alexander inherited the title in 1685 before it passed, in turn to his eldest son, another Sir William who became the 3rd Baronet in 1701. Interestingly, William's daughter Margory married Reverend James Gilliland, minister of the kirk and it is even more interesting to know that a several times, great-grandson of that couple, Andrew Dowlen-Gilliland lives in the area, at Mersington House a little to the south of Purves Hall, such a lovely link with the past.

In 1730, Sir William's son, yet another William, married Lady Anne, daughter of Alexander Hume-Campbell, 2nd Earl Marchmont, a marriage which would ultimately see the Purves Baronets moving away from Purves Hall to reside at the great house of Marchmont. William's and Anne's son became the 5th Baronet in 1762 before the Greenlaw 'legend', Sir William Hume-Campbell-Purves was installed 6th Baronet, having assumed the 'Hume-Campbell' part of his name from his mother.

- Purves Hall – Redbraes Castle -

It was he who inherited Marchmont from his grandmother Anne's brother, Hugh, 3rd Earl of Marchmont, 3rd Lord Polwarth.

There were another two Baronets of Purves Hall, Sir Hugh Purves-Hume-Campbell, the 7th Baronet from 1833 until 1894 and finally the 8th and last, Sir John Home-Purves-Hume-Campbell from 1894 until his death in 1960 when the line failed thus ending a long and distinguished line of Purves lairds at Greenlaw. Happily, as intimated a modern day member, on a direct line from the 3rd Baronet is still amongst his ain folk deep in the heart of Berwickshire.

- Redbraes Castle -

It is unclear when Redbraes was originally built but the ruins we now see, formed part of a magnificent, three towered frontage with the central, entrance tower the most impressive. Each tower was topped by a pointed dome roof and were connected by the main block. The two wing towers, each of five storeys high, contained two windows to the front at each level while the narrower though taller, six storey, central tower, contained a line of single windows. There appeared, on the central tower, an entrance, almost certainly to a courtyard, which was surrounded by more walls and smaller towers. That particular building was said to be built in the 16th century to replace an earlier tower which was originally built by the St. Clairs of Herdmanstoun in East Lothian who were prominent in the area at that time, particularly at Polwarth.

That family were the Barons of Polwarth until the mid 15th century when Margaret St. Clair carried the lands and title to the Hume family on her marriage to Patrick of that ilk in 1451. It would appear, Redbraes was not erected until the Humes became the predominant family of the area though a tower house had been built before the destruction of Polwarth Castle by the Earl of Hertford during his 'visit' of 1545 causing the family to take up residence at Redbraes before undertaking major works as described above, towards the end of the 16th century. The family, the Humes and Hume-Campbells lived at Redbraes for nearly two centuries gaining title, Lord Polwarth and Earl of Marchmont during that time.

*T*he 1st Earl of Marchmont, Sir Patrick Hume was an interesting character and has gone down in Scottish history as one of the most famous of all Covenanters, a strong and vociferous defender of the Scottish Church. He was born in 1641, the latest arrival in a very Presbyterian family, and attended school and university in Edinburgh studying law, later working in Paris before his long awaited return to Scotland. So zealous were his beliefs, he was imprisoned but his 'main claim to fame' was still to follow.

Remains of Redbraes Castle
Courtesy and Copyright @2012 Becky Williamson

*O*n release from prison, his freedom was short lived when he was implicated in the *Rye House Plot* of 1683, a plan to assassinate King

Charles II and his brother, James, Duke of York. Patrick first went in to hiding, before returning home but had to hide in the family crypt at Polwarth Kirk where his daughter, Grizell, arrived every day from Redbraes Castle, with fresh food. So often did the young lady walk up the hill from Redbraes Castle to serve her father, that trodden path became known as the Lady's Walk. Finally Sir Patrick had to flee to the continent where he became known as Dr. Wallace but made his triumphant return to Britain with the forces of William of Orange at the so called Glorious Revolution of 1688. Patrick was then made Lord Chancellor to the king and received many honours and title including the afore mentioned lordship of Polwarth and Earldom of Marchmont.

Polwarth Kirk

*T*he 2nd Lord Polwarth and Earl of Marchmont, was Alexander, Sir Patrick's eldest surviving son who assumed the extra name, Campbell upon his marriage to Margaret, daughter and heiress of the Campbell estate in Cessnock, Ayrshire. He became an advocate after studying law at Utrecht and later ascended to the bench as Lord Cessnock. That couple's daughter, Lady Anne Hume-Campbell, married Sir William, 4th Baronet of Purves Hall and Greenlaw. In later times, Alexander was Britain's ambassador to Denmark before entering the House of Lords. He planned to build a new house at Marchmont but the cost was more then he could afford or was willing to spend, however that task was undertaken by his son Hugh who was an ever so benevolent supporter of the people, town and parish of Greenlaw.

- Marchmont House -

*I*n 1750, work on the great house began and was completed three years later. Hugh's father had plans drawn up by William Adam but the house was ultimately designed and built in the Palladian style by local architect, Thomas Gibson who, many believe, worked closely to the Adam style. Indeed some say he used the Adam prototype in his design but that is probably a little unfair even though the Adam style is very evident.

*W*hile the family made the move from Redbraes, the old castle was not entirely neglected and was used for more than a century thereafter, mainly as offices and storage though the towers were allowed to fall apart.

*T*he Earldom of Marchmont lapsed on the death of Hugh, 3rd Earl since he had no sons, but the subsidiary title of Lord Polwarth is still extant in the shape of Andrew Walter Hepburne-Scott of Harden, the 11th Lord, who lives at his family seat, Harden House in Roxburghshire.

*O*f course, the Purves-Hume-Campbell Baronets were, as we have seen, bequeathed the house and estate but they sold Marchmont to the McEwen family just before the outset of the First World War. That family made huge alterations to the house including adding what is now the top floor, connecting the pavilions at either end of the house and building a grand, double storey music room in what was the stable block in the north pavilion. That room contained a great organ and organ pipes which would not have looked out of place in a great cathedral.

Marchmont House

Marchmont House, the rear or west elevation
©2007 Mark J. Reynold – Wikipedia – see acknowledgements

*T*he house, as we have seen, which was originally designed and built in the William Adam style, by Robert Gibson but the building we now see, is, to a large degree, the works of Robert Lorimer, a great friend of John Helius Finnie McEwan. Lorimer also performed minor miracles at the family's other home at Bardrochat in Ayrshire. Marchmont is simply one of the most beautiful buildings in Scotland and the interior more than matches the exterior for beauty and heavenly craftsmanship. Indeed many experts believe, the interior of Marchmont House is, by far, the most lavish and architecturally supreme building of its kind...anywhere. In particular, the period plasterwork is unsurpassed having been carried out by the master of masters, Thomas Clayton, who worked on many Adam buildings. He was also responsible for the plaster work at Hamilton Palace, Blair Castle and the Royal apartments at the Palace of Holyroodhouse. He was a genius in his field of art work and has long since been recognised as one of the world's great 18th century craftsmen.

*S*ir John Helius Finnie McEwan, a Conservative politician who served as Under-Secretary of State for Scotland in the early years of World II, was created 1st Baronet of Marchmont and Badrochat in

Ayrshire in 1953 but died only nine years later, leaving the Baronetcy to his son Sir James who, like his father, held the title for only nine years before he too, died at the young age of 47.

Marchmont Doo'cot – courtesy of Walter Baxter

*T*he estates and title then passed to his brother Sir Robert but once again, Robert, the 3rd Baronet held the title for only nine years before he too passed away, at age 56. Sir Robert's wife Brigid Cecilia, Lady McEwan, mother of the next two Baronets, still lives at Polwarth to the present day and is a very highly regarded lady, friend and supporter of Greenlaw as she has been, since her arrival in the region, she too is a much deserved notable of the old town.

*H*er elder son, Sir James, succeeded his father in 1980 but died barely three years later aged just 22 such a sad loss at so young an age. James was succeeded by his younger brother, Sir John Roderick Hugh McEwan 5th Baronet, who still lives at the family home at Bardrochat and is considered the putative Chief of the Clan McEwen. That is to say, there is no clan chief at present, the clan has never had a chief, but Sir John is the likely 'front runner' for that post if ever it comes to pass.

Marchmont House

*T*he McEwens left Marchmont around 1980 before it came in to the hands of the Sue Ryder Foundation but that foundation no longer practices there and in more recent times, Marchmont has lain, sadly, empty and now looking so lost and forlorn. It is believed however, to be back in private hands with the new owners planning to return the great masterpiece to a private residence.

*I*t is more than distressing to see one of Scotland's great houses lie, as it is, empty and appearing unloved but, hopefully, if the new owners can return the old lady to her former glories, it would be a priceless asset long in to the future.

*T*he great estate also contains so many other fine buildings, apart from the great house, all architectural gems amidst one the most beautifully laid out estates including the walled gardens and the longest tree lined avenue in Scotland. The estate even had its very own railway station on the Berwickshire Line which connected the East Coast Mainline and the old Waverley Line. Closed to passengers in 1951, the railways carried on with freight trains until 1965 when it closed forever but the station house, now a private home, and railway platform still remain.

*M*archmont is not accessed by a main road but it is accessible. It lies some five kilometres to the north-east of Greenlaw but less than four km almost due south of Polwarth. It must be said however, while the great house and estate were in the old parish of Polwarth, it was to Greenlaw, the larger and more important community, where they extended their arms, their influence and to a greater degree, their benevolence.

Blackadder is a byword in Greenlaw including the river,

**and..........
The Blackadder
Holiday Park**

**Blackadder
Hotel**

**The
Masonic
Lodge
Blackadder
no.1350 and
Blackadder Social
Club**

....Not forgetting, the Blackadder Mini Market

- Greenlaw -

Greenlaw – local descendants of the old aristocratic families

*T*he local lairds, most of whom have gone to a better place, have left their names and marks on the old town but we are blessed by the fact we still have some of their descendants in our midst.

*F*irst of all, there is Andrew Dowlen-Gilliland who lives at Mersington to the south, a several times great grandson of James Gilliland who became minister of the kirk in 1712 and his wife, Marjory Purves who's father, Sir Alexander was the 5th Baronet of Purves Hall. Andrew is formerly an officer in the Royal Marines, a company director and is also active in charitable work. The Marchmont connection comes in the shape of Lady Brigid McEwan, a gracious lady as we have seen, who has great affinity with the town but now lives in Polwarth while members of the ancient and noble family of Home still reside at Old Greenlaw in the shape of Felicity Douglas-Home and her son, Peregrine. That wonderful lady like Lady Brigid McEwan, is held in the townspeople's highest affections.

*B*efore we take our leave of Greenlaw, let us have a look at some more very old photographs of the town and the way things were in the days of our forebears.

The way things were...

Above : Marchmont when still a family home
Below : The Blackadder Hotel when no alcohol was served

both courtesy of Carol Trotter

....but some are no more

LEVEL CROSSING, GREENLAW.

Above : A level crossing on the A697 south of Easter Bridge
Below : 'In Jail' but only visiting after the prison had closed

Both courtesy of Carol Trotter

- Greenlaw -

- A Parting of Ways -

Now it is time to go back to where it all started, on the old Kirk Hill, where a gracious old lady has stood for more than 850 years, looking over and surveying the community. She has witnessed good, more especially those of the parish...and the bad, predominately foreign intruders who arrived with death and destruction on their on their minds and at the end of their pikes and swords. It is with those words and thoughts I step through the church gates just as another thought comes to mind while looking over the town centre and it is not difficult to see why Greenlaw was such an important place and indeed still is...the history of the old lady will ensure that.

There is a good, solid, permanent feel all around and I cannot help but think, that air of importance and confidence still exists in the old county town, one of the most historic in Southern Scotland and maybe one day soon, that importance will return, hopefully in the form of more industry and jobs but do not tell the local people their town is not still important though, just as it is; for them, of course, it is the most important place in the Borders.

The many visitors who arrive at the Blackadder Holiday Park for their annual holiday, or others just visiting, would, I am sure, endorse that sentiment with friends on a day out on the bowling green, an evening in the Blackadder Hotel or Cross Keys, coffee at Poppy's or a meal at the restaurant. They are the places where the inquisitive visitor, like me, is able to learn more of the local history, handed down over generations from father to son or even mother to daughter. A walk from the Wester Bridge to the Easter is a walk along one of the oldest High Streets in the county and passing below the kirk, county hall, mercat cross and War Memorial simply confirms that.

Take a pause on the Easter Bridge and watch the gushing waters of the Blackadder flow away from Greenlaw. That scene has the power to evoke all forms of emotion, happiness, joy, glee or sadness; happy to watch the waters rush in gay abandon towards her meeting with old friends and the joy of entering the safety of the bosom that is the North Sea. Or you may view the sight of the departing waters as the end, the finish of a great journey through the history of a wonderful old town and parish, yet it's not, it is just another beginning. That beginning begins here and now with a peaceful walk through the Happer Memorial Woodlands, on the banks of the river, back to where it all began at Wester Bridge. That is where the Blackadder Water flows triumphantly in to her spiritual home, Greenlaw, the ancient County Town still exuding a powerful beat, deep in the heart of the old County of Berwick.

Now where was I? Oh yes! I remember, I was busy working on a story of Duns and district when I was blissfully distracted...................... I must get back over the Greenlaw Moor road to Old Dunse and take up where I left off.

Greenlaw

Blackadder Water flowing east under the Easter Bridge then passing by Marchmont Road on her way to pastures new

Until we meet again, Greenlaw

Fare thee weel

- Bibliography -

*An Old Berwickshire Town, History of the Town and Parish of Greenlaw, from the earliest times to the present day – Robert Gibson, edited by his son, Thomas Gibson. Oliver & Boyd, Tweeddale Court, Edinburgh – 1905

*Churches and Churchyards of Berwickshire – James Robson – J & J.H. Rutherford, Kelso – 1891

*The Road Tae Grinlae – Robert R. Young, Edited & Illustrated by his son, Russell J. Young. Dolphin Press, Gelnrothes, Fife – 1996

*Greenlaw – Borders Family History Society – Elspeth Ewan and Carol Trotter ISBN 1 874232 08 5 – MD Print and Design, Edinburgh – 1996.

*The Churches and Churchyards of Berwickshire – G.A.C. Binnie. ISBN 978-0952 608505 – Dr. G.A.C. Binnie. Ladykirk, Norham - 1995

*History of Berwickshire's Towns and Villages To The Present Day – Elizabeth M. W. Layhe. ISBN 979-0952 322 108 - EnTire Productions – 1994

*Village Kirks of the Borders of Scotland – James Denham. ISBN 978 1447 743 934 – Lulu Publishing, Raleigh, NC, USA. - 2011

*Childhood Memories – John Goodfellow, Greenlaw.

*People of Medieval Scotland, 1093-1314 – www.poms.ac.uk (accessed on many occasions between March and May, 2015)

*Greenlaw berwick-freecen.webspace/virginmedia/com/Greenlaw/Grenlaw.htm

*Stravaiging Scotland website – stravaiging.com

*Site details for Marchmont House & Estate - canmore.rchams.gov.uk/en/site/58500/details

*Marchmont and the Humes of Polwarth – Julian Margaret Maitland Warrender – William Blackwood and Sons, Edinburgh – 1894

*Site details for Purves Hall - www.britishlistedbuildings.co.uk/sc-4144-purves-hall-tower-eccles

*Town Hall Website – www.greenlawtownhall.bordernet.co.uk

*Pigot and Co's Directory of 1826

Notes

Notes